# RUMI

## AND HIS SUFI PATH OF LOVE

# RUMI

## AND HIS SUFI PATH OF LOVE

Edited by
M. Fatih Çıtlak and Hüseyin Bingül

*The Light*

New Jersey

Published by The Light, Inc.
26 Worlds Fair Dr. Unit C
Somerset, New Jersey, 08873, USA


www.thelightpublishing.com


Library of Congress Cataloging-in-Publication Data

Rumi and his Sufi path of love / edited by M. Fatih Citlak and Huseyin Bingul.
    p. cm.
Includes bibliographical references and index.
ISBN-13: 978-1-59784-078-1
1.  Jalal al-Din Rumi, Maulana, 1207-1273. 2.  Mevleviyeh. 3.  Sufism--
Doctrines.  I. Citlak, M. Fatih. II. Bingul, Huseyin.
BP189.7.M42R86 2007
297.4092--dc22
                                        2007002853


Printed by
Victor Graphics
Baltimore, Maryland

# TABLE OF CONTENTS

# CONTRIBUTORS

- MEHMET ŞEKER – Author and researcher, Australia.

- M. FETHULLAH GÜLEN - Islamic scholar, thinker, and author of numerous books translated to different languages, who has inspired millions to take part in a movement of intercultural and interfaith dialogue and educational activism.

- DR. RAMAZAN ALTINTAŞ – Professor of *Kalam* (Islamic Theology and Philosophy) at Cumhuriyet University, Sivas.

- DR. SEEMA ARIF – Professor of Behavioral Sciences at the University of Central Punjab, Lahore, Pakistan.

- DR. MICHAELA M. ÖZELSEL – Professor of Psychology, Germany.

- DR. ADNAN KARAİSMAİLOĞLU – Chair, Department of Persian Language and Literature, Kırıkkale University, Kırıkkale.

- ÜLKER ERKE – Mevlevi miniature artist.

- NURİYE AKMAN – Journalist for *Zaman* Daily.

- DR. SELAHATTİN HİDAYETOĞLU – Retired professor of Turkish-Islamic Literature and a descendent of Rumi of the 21st generation.

- DR. SEZAİ KÜÇÜK – Deputy Dean of the School of Theology at Sakarya University, Sakarya.

- DR. NURİ ŞİMŞEKLER – Director of Rumi Studies at Selçuk University, Konya.

- ERDOĞAN EROL – Director of Mawlana Museum, Konya, Turkey.

- PETER H. CUNZ – Mevlevi Postnishin and Director of the Department of Rational Utilization of Energy, Swiss Federal Office of Energy.

- ŞEFİK CAN – The late *Masnavi* reciter and Mevlevi spiritual head (*sar-tariq*), who authored nine books on Rumi as well as on poetry and classical mythology.

- DR. ABDULLAH ÖZTÜRK – Deputy Dean of the Faculty of Arts and Science at Selçuk University, Konya.

# INTRODUCTION

For centuries, Rumi has been speaking in his works to people from various cultures and backgrounds through the language of love. Rumi, as he is most commonly known in the West, or "Mawlana" in the East, is one of the few people who have exerted a great influence over space and time. Rumi speaks directly to the hearts and transcends the boundaries of time. As one of the most published poets in the West, Rumi builds bridges of understanding between the Islamic world and the West, and his work represents common ground for dialogue.

In the effort to promote Rumi and his Sufi path to the West, UNESCO not only declared that 2007 will be "Rumi Year," but also announced that the Mevlevi Sama Ceremony has been accepted as a Masterpiece of the Oral Tradition of the Intangible Heritage of Humanity, which is an international distinction destined to raise public awareness of the value of this heritage.

The whirling dervishes have been whirling during the Sama Ceremony for centuries accompanied by the verses of Rumi, who anticipated, in fact, that his works would one day cross all boundaries:

> *I silently moaned so that for a hundred centuries to come,*
> *The world would echo in the sound of my hayhâ*[1]
> *It would turn on axis of my hayhât.*[2]

It is now 800 years later; people from all over the world are reading Rumi more than ever; he is well-known as a Sufi saint-poet in

---

[1]  The words "*hayhâ*" and "*hayhât*" are different uses of the same term meaning "alas" or "woe to me!"

[2]  Rumi, *Divan-i Kabir*, Ghazal No: 562/7.

the East following the path toward God primarily by means of love, and Westerners find his Sufi path of love the most appealing.

Having captured the hearts of so many people in the West, the words of this great Sufi cleric sends hope for the dark times we are living in. Rumi's sweet-songed reed is needed to draw away the increasing sensuous drumbeats of the so-called inevitable clash of civilizations. At this time in history, it is most imperative that we find the time to come together, to talk and try to understand one another, to find common ground and shared references. Once again, eight centuries later, we need this outstanding poet, a revered mystic renowned for his understanding and wide-reaching embrace, to shed light on the interrelations of human beings. For every word from his mouth is full of love and peace. His words are addressed to all humans and to all humanity.

This collection of articles brings together social scientists, Islamic scholars, academics, philosophers, and psychologists from an unparalleled geographic range. Organized around four themes, this collection provides the reader with a glimpse of Rumi's universal message. Together, the authors underscore the exemplary atmosphere built by Rumi; an atmosphere where the values of compassion and tolerance are respected and where the doors to dialogue are opened.

The first section, "Discovering Rumi Today," contains selections that deal with how Rumi's message of love transcends the boundaries of time and space and why he is a necessary voice to build bridges of understanding between the contemporary East and West. The lead article by Mehmet Şeker, "Rumi's Path of Love and 'Being Freed' with the Sama," provides a macro perspective on Rumi's address to all humanity through his works which together present the common bond of humanity with a timeless message of love. The author also provides a general introduction to Rumi's interpretation of the whirling prayer. The venerable Fethullah Gülen's erudite and comprehensive analysis of the extent and vitality of Rumi's influence describes how Rumi hastened toward God and how he evoked similar yearnings in countless others to embark on spiritual journeys throughout the ages. Prof. Ramazan Altıntaş' analysis of Rumi's perception of human scrutinizes the unique position of humankind in the whole universe as the recipient of God's Attributes. Prof. Seema Arif, in her analysis of "The Memetic Counseling of Masnavi," examines how Rumi's poetic genius in the Masnavi successfully handles modern discourse techniques and achieves a universal language communicable to people of all ages across time. In the last article of this section, "Rumi Resonates through the Ages," Prof. Michaela M. Özelsel introduces readers to Rumi's psychological counseling in his Fihi ma Fihi, demonstrating its originality and applicability in modern medicine.

The second section, "The life of Rumi and Mevlevi Sufism," starts with Rumi's biography. Casting some light on the family of Rumi journeying westward from present-day Afghanistan to the Seljuk capital of Konya, in present-day Turkey, Prof. Adnan Karaismailoğlu provides us with a brief account of the times and life of Rumi, including the influence of his father, his teachers, and the spiritual importance of Shams of Tabriz during the formative development of this remarkable spiritual teacher and poet. Journalist Nuriye Akman's interview with Şefik Can, the late Masnavi reciter and Mevlevi spiritual head, underlines the centrality of the Qur'an and the Prophet Muhammad in Rumi's life and clarifies certain misunderstandings surrounding him. In the third article of this section, Prof. Selahattin Hidayetoğlu, a 21st century descendent of Rumi, provides a lucid summary of Sufi basics in his article on "Rumi and Sufism." Prof. Sezai Küçük's detailed analysis of the Sama ceremony demonstrates the wide scope of spiritual signs of the whirling dervishes' prayer. Prof. Nuri Şimşekler, the director of Rumi Studies of Selçuk University, provides us with the historical keystones by which Mevlevi Sufism traveled from the Seljuk capital city of Konya to the Balkans, Central Asia, and North African Ottoman territories. The article also casts some light on contemporary Mevlevi Sufism and how this tradition has developed since its inception in 1273. In this section's final article, Erdoğan Erol, the director of Mawlana Museum in Konya, introduces the reader to the main Mevlevi Center where Rumi is buried next to his father Bahaaddin Muhammad, who was himself renown as the Sultan of Scholars, and provides the reader with a tour of the outer and interior sections of the center, which was converted into a museum in 1926.

The third section, "Rumi in the West," includes contributions from various scholars that attempt to analyze the Western audiences' understanding of this remarkable saint poet and his Sufi path. In his enlightening and judicious account of "Mawlana from a European Point of View," Peter H. Cunz, the Swiss Mevlevi head, discusses the reasons for Rumi's attraction to audiences in Europe as well as the contemporary Europeans' strong appeal with Rumi's Sufi way. Şefik Can summarizes Western scholarship on Rumi and Sufism evaluating the works of western scholars who have brought Rumi's voice and breath to the West in his article of "Rumi studies in the West." In an article on the French scholar Eva de Vitray Meyerovitch's contributions to the promotion of Rumi, Prof. Abdullah Öztürk analyzes how Meyerovitch has successfully presented Rumi's poetic talent and spiritual essence to Western audiences.

The last section attempts to hold up a candle to Rumi's poetry and strives to illustrate how his work has raised literary and spiritual consciousness for audiences around the world. This particular section starts with the rhyming translation of "The Song of the Reed." This is the first story of Rumi's Masnavi and the accompanying musical notation of the opening lines of "The Song of the Reed," the sacred musical heritage of the Mevlevi Sufism and a masterpiece of Ottoman Turkish music. In his inspiring and meditative critique of "The Song of the Reed," Hüseyin Bingül discusses how the poetic genius pours his own heart out and takes the audience far back in time to the creation of humankind through the metaphor of the reed-flute that longs to return to the reed-bed from where it was uprooted, like the lover passionately yearning for the beloved. This last section concludes with Rumi's poetic "Seven Pieces of Advice" and other maxims of him that resonate with countless people today.

The completion of this project would not have been possible if it were not for the contributions of H. Nur Artıran (*Masnavi* reciter), Dr. Cihan Okuyucu (Turkish Language and Literature Department Chairperson, Fatih University), and Dr. H. Ali Yurtsever (President of Rumi Forum, Washington DC). To each of these people we owe our sincere gratitude.

M. Fatih Çıtlak and Hüseyin Bingül
Istanbul, 2007

# PART I

---

## Discovering Rumi Today

# RUMI'S PATH OF LOVE AND "BEING FREED" WITH THE SAMA

Mehmet Şeker

Human beings are equipped in the best possible way, both materially and spiritually. Potentially, a human being is able to achieve the level of "the best of creation," which is dependent on his ability to use and develop his endowment of spiritual attributes. Those who can escape from the material world and escalate toward the higher ranks of the heart and soul will experience this world in a different way, and they will become conscious of the secrets of creation. When they look, they will see things that others cannot; and everywhere they look, they will see the manifestations of the Beautiful Names of God. Without doubt, they would never trade such moments filled with the indescribable flavors of spiritualism for anything. Instead, they will spend all the bounties given to them for the sake of God with the sole intention of reaching Him. Those who have achieved such nearness to God are always careful in their relations with the Beloved and thus extremely cautious to retain their sensitivity and maintain this level. These people are nothing more or less, in effect, than Friends of the Truth.

Mawlana Jalaladdin Rumi is one of these Friends—one of the perfect representatives of the many Sufi devotees whose way of life is to love and be of service to people, to become a perfect human being, and thus to have the good pleasure of God. Rumi's path of love within Sufism's inclusiveness has always attracted people from all cultures and backgrounds, and this is certainly the major reason for Rumi's appeal in both the East and the West.

The theoretical aspect of this path is Sufism, while the practical aspect is *Dervishood*. Rumi led the theoretical path, as a leader for his time and all times to come after him; in addition, his mature

*dervishood*, taken from this world and decorated with angelic qualities, set a good example of devotion to God through the passion
and love with which he inspired millions. During his lifetime, there
were many people of other faiths around Rumi, listening to him
and respecting him for what he was teaching. Thus, Rumi emerged
in a period in which disorders, conflicts and exploitation lay heavy
on the peoples of the world. Throughout this period, Rumi proved
himself to be both a powerful personality and an eminent scholar.
For not only did he talk about compassion and tolerance, but he actually produced an exemplary atmosphere where these values were
upheld, thereby opening the door to dialogue through his message.

Today, we are experiencing rather similar turmoil, unrest and
conflicts everywhere. Yet instead of raising the awareness of the need
for understanding, religious devotions are simply being manipulated
in the so-called "clash of civilizations." Once again, therefore, we need
this most outstanding poet, a revered mystic renowned for his understanding and wide embrace, to shed light on the relation of human
beings to their Creator as well as their interrelations with others.

## THE EAST AND WEST'S FASCINATION WITH RUMI

The world has never been without representatives of love and peace.
Rumi was and is one of the perfect representatives of such a complete human being, and one of the greatest teachers of universal
love and peace.

Sama Ceremony. Photo courtesy of Rumi Forum, Washington, DC

Rumi has always been a major figure in the Middle East and Western Asia, where he has had an exalted and comprehensive impact among a wide variety of people. The great Islamic scholar and poet, Muhammad Iqbal, became fascinated with Rumi's view of discovering the Divine Entrustment in one's self. Embracing Rumi's understanding of the perfect human being, and seeing Rumi as a spiritual guide for himself, Iqbal states, "I received a share of his light and warmth. My night has become day due to his star...In Rumi, there is sorrow, a burning that is not strange to us. His union talks of going beyond the separations. One feels the beauty of love in his reed and receives a share, a blessing from the Greatness of God."[1]

Yet Rumi is not merely a *Mawlana* ("our master")—one of the titles assigned to him and widely used among Muslims—whose scope is limited to one part of the world. Rather, he is the master of people from both the East and the West. In fact, Westerners have increasingly been amazed that his presence seems so alive eight centuries after his death. In a tribute to Rumi, Andrew Harvey puts forward that Rumi, the remote star shining in the west, will help lead the west out of its materialist manifestation of ego-over-everything. Thus, Harvey sees Rumi as "an essential guide to the new mystical renaissance that is struggling to be born today...and the spiritual inspiration for the 21st century."[2]

Rumi was born in Balkh, Khorasan, (present-day Uzbekistan, Turkmenistan, Afghanistan, Tajikistan, and Iran), the home which he and his family left at the age of five. The very mystical foundations of Mevlevi Sufism were, actually, laid as a result of the fusion of the Khorasan school of Sufism, which began entering Anatolia at regular intervals from the early thirteenth century onward, with Seljuk culture. Rumi's family likewise journeyed to Anatolia, in present-day Turkey, where Rumi composed all his works and spent most of his adult life. Here, in the Seljuk Turks' cosmopolitan capital city of Konya, he resided until he passed away on December 17, 1273.

---

[1]    Iqbal, Muhammad, *Armagan-i Hijaz* (Gift from Hijaz), Lahore, 1938.
[2]    Harvey, Andrew, *The Way of Passion: A Celebration of Rumi*, Frog Ltd, CA, 1994.

It is narrated that he had requested his funeral prayer to be lead by Sheikh Sadraddin of Konya. When the Sheikh came to the front for the prayer, Tabib Akmaladdin warned the people by saying, "Mind your manners and be respectful. He was the Sultan of the true sheikhs; that is who has passed away." Sheikh Sadraddin, after hearing this, was moved to tears and could not continue with the prayer. So instead, Qadi Sirajaddin led the prayer.[3] People from various religions, cultures and backgrounds honored him at his funeral. Local Muslims, Christians, Jews, Turks, Arabs, Persians, and Romans all followed the bier of this lover of God.

The Mevlevi dervishes have kept the date he died as a festival, which is called *Shab-i Arus*, because Rumi, a true devotee of God, saw life as a corridor for meeting with God, and defined death as the meeting time, which he described in this poem:

*On the day of death, when my coffin is on the move,*
*Do not suppose I have any pain at leaving this world.*
*When you see my hearse, say not*
*"Leaving! He's leaving!"*
*That time will be for me union and encounter.*
*When you commit me to the grave,*
*Say not "Farewell! Farewell,"*
*For the grave is a veil over the reunion of Paradise.*

Being a Sufi, Rumi deserted his false self and all illusion on the way to perfection, ultimately aiming to reach God, and he always had a well-grounded and profound interpretation of the teachings of the Prophet of Islam, peace be upon him, and the Qur'an in his works:

*I am the servant of the Qur'an as long as I have life.*
*I am the dust on the path of Muhammad, the Chosen One.*
*If anyone interprets my words in any other way,*
*I deplore that person and I deplore his words.*[4]

---

3  Çelebi, Asaf, *Hayat Mecmuasi*, 1960.
4  Rumi, *Divan-i Kabir*, Quatrain No. 1173.5 See Rumi, Masnavi, Vol. VI, 2900-2904.

Rumi's love and awe for God, combined with his poetic character, blossom in *Masnavi*. Rumi was in his fifties when he started *Masnavi*, a work which he completed in eight years. Apart from his *Masnavi*, written in rhyming couplets, Rumi has four other major works: *Divan-i Kabir* is lyrical, and the other three are prose. With more than forty thousand couplets, *Divan-i Kabir* is full of an enthusiasm and awe that reflects the inner spiritual world of Rumi. The works in prose are: *Fihi ma Fihi* which contains Rumi's teachings to his students and the public on various topics; *Majalis-i Sab'a,* which contains his sermons; and *Maktubat,* which contains his letters to various people.

For centuries, Rumi, the remote star, has been speaking to people from diverse faith communities, cultures and backgrounds through the language of love. He has opened up his blessed heart to all those who find something of themselves in his words. And it is now 800 years later, people from all over the world are reading Rumi more than ever.

## RUMI AND THE *SAMA*

The "*Sama*" (whirling dance) symbolizes many exquisite aspects of life: the creation of the universe; the creation of human beings; our birth into this world; the progress of human beings after the realization of servanthood, as supported with the love of God; and our escalation toward the ranks of perfected human (*insan-i kamil*).

As for the emergence of the *Sama,* it is reported that one day Rumi was passing in front of his friend Salahaddin Zarqubi's jewelry shop, in Konya. In the shop, Zarqubi was shaping gold by hammering it in rhythm. Enraptured by the rhythmic sounds of the hammer used by Zarkubi, Rumi said:

> *The souls that have clung to water and clay,*
> *Are pleased on being freed from them,*
> *And begin to dance in the air and breezes of love,*
> *Becoming perfected like the full moon.*

Seeing the manifestations of the Beloved's Beautiful Names everywhere, what this great mystic heard in the hammering of gold was the very word Allah, Al-lah, Al-lah in the rhythmic sound, and it inspired him into a state of ecstasy which resulted in his *sama,* or whirling.

Rumi, whose spirit was already full of love and awe of God, was able to discern the "universal movement" of creation as he raised his hands towards the sky and started to turn round on his own axis, while also moving in orbit in a state of awe throughout his *sama.* For Rumi, the rapture and attraction of all existence, from the smallest atoms to the largest celestial objects, is due to a hidden attraction to the Divine.[5] During *sama,* his excitement was great with the emotion of intoxication, imbibed from the wine of the All-Loving. The following poem of Rumi's expresses how he understood the *sama*:

> *What is Sama, do you know?*
> *It is hearing the sound of "yes,"*
> *Of separating one from himself and reaching the Lord,*
> *Seeing and knowing the state of the Friend,*
> *And hearing, through the divine veils, the secrets of the Lord.*
> *What is Sama, do you know?*
> *Being ignorant of existence and tasting eternity in the*
> *ultimate mortality.*
> *What is Sama, do you know?*
> *Struggling with the carnal soul; fluttering on the ground*
> *like a half-slain hen.*
> *What is Sama, do you know?*
> *Feeling the cure of Prophet Jacob, and sensing the arrival of Prophet*
> *Joseph from the scent of a shirt.*
> *What is Sama, do you know?*
> *Like the staff of Prophet Moses, it is swallowing all the tricks of the*
> *Pharaoh's magicians.*
> *What is Sama, do you know?*
> *Opening the heart like Shams-i Tabrizi [an excellent devotee],*
> *And seeing the Divine light.*

---

5    See Rumi, *Masnavi,* Vol. VI, 2900-2904.

## THE *SAMA* AND CONTEMPLATION

The *Sama* is contemplation in action. Contemplation was initially carried out silently in the inner self. Under the enlightenment of *hadiths* (sayings of the Prophet Muhammad, peace be upon him) which warn not to contemplate on the essence of God Himself, for God in His essence cannot be comprehended, meditation came to be focused on the manifestations and actions of God. As an aid to meditation and to minimize any outside interference during periods of profound thought, simple, rhythmic sounds were used to induce a meditative state intent on the love of God. At first, only natural sounds were used, but with time, the sounds of different musical instruments with spiritual essences were introduced into the *Sama*.

In the early days, usually the *nay* (the reed-flute), *rabab* (the three-stringed violin), *daf* (the tambourine with cymbals), and *zurna* (a woodwind instrument) were used, but over time, only the *nay* and *rabab* survived.

Music is defined by Rumi in the following couplet:

> *Music is the nutrition of the souls of the servants of the Lord,*
> *Since, in music, there is the hope of reaching God.*

Therefore, music, when combined with mediation and contemplation, is seen as being a faster way to reaching God. On the other hand, music brings out physical movement, as it addresses bodily impulses and desires. At first, these motions were restricted to the swinging of the body while seated. However, with time, people started to accompany the musical harmony with swaying and larger movements, and this gradually evolved into the *Sama*. In this way, contemplation became the union of the soul, sound, and motion, as both the heart and body achieved a state of meditation, overcoming all physical and intellectual interference.

Thus, the *Sama* symbolizes the escalation of the human spirit: the servant's turning of his face toward the Truth; being exalted with Divine love; abandoning personal identity and the self to become lost in God; and finally returning to servanthood, mature and purified.

The *Samazan*, the whirling dervish, with the *sikka* (the traditional "hat") on his head, and with the *tannura* (a shroud-like gown) on his body, is born into the truth as he symbolically removes his jacket at the onset of the dance, and begins his revolutions—thus, his evolution—on the path of profound contemplation. During *Sama*, his arms are wide open, with his right hand turned toward the sky as if praying, ready to receive honor from the Divine One, and his left hand turned down, transferring the bounties that come from the Lord to those who are willing to receive them. As the *Samazan* whirls from right to left, circling with the full devotion of his heart, he embraces all the nations of the world, and all of creation, with the utmost love and respect.

Ultimately, humanity was created to love and to be loved. According to Rumi, all types of love are bridges to Divine love, and believing this completely, Rumi spent his whole life dedicated to God Almighty. Not only did he try to reach the Lord himself, but he earnestly strove to help others to do the same. In the end, he was a traveler on the journey of love, describing this love as one that "did not leave anything of me, nor on me." And through these travels of the soul, he allowed his feelings and emotions be heard by countless others, leaving a powerful trail of inspiration that would long outlast his own life, and come to nurture millions of souls.

# JALALADDIN RUMI

M. Fethullah Gülen

There are some significant personalities who with the help of their voice and breath, their love and excitement, and their promise for humanity always remain fresh and alive over the course of centuries. Time evidently fails to make these characters obsolete. Their thoughts, analyses, explanations, and spiritual messages, which will never be lost, represent, ever anew, alternative solutions and prescriptions for today's social problems, in great variety and diversity.

Rumi is one such personality. Despite the vast amount of time that separates his life from ours, Rumi continues to hear and to listen to us, to share our feelings, to present solutions to our problems in a voice that is without equal. Despite the fact that he lived some centuries ago, he remains absolutely alive among and with us today. He is a man of light-one who receives his light from the spirit of the Master of Humanity (Prophet Muhammad, peace and blessings be upon him), distributing this light in a variety of manners to just about everywhere. He was chosen to be one of the world's saints and to be pure of heart; a blessed one whose words are outstanding among those of the heroes of love and passion. He was and continues to function as Israfil; blowing life into dead spirits. He did and continues to provide the water of life to the barren hearts of many; a spiritual irrigation. He was and continues to provide light for the travelers on their paths. He was and continues to be the perfect heir of the Prophet.

Jalaladdin Rumi, a man of God, hastened toward God on his own spiritual journey; but in addition to this he evoked similar journeys in countless others-journeys marked by an eager striving toward God. He was a balanced man of ecstasy who sprang alive with love and excitement; he did this to such an extent that he inspired in others these significant feelings; he continues to do so. In addition to his passion for God, along with his knowledge and love of Him, Rumi is further renowned as a hero in terms of both his respect and fear of God. He was and continues to be one who beckons; whose powerful voice invites everyone to the truth and the ultimate blessed reality. Rumi was an inclusive master whose joy was a direct consequence of His joy, whose love and passion were the result of His special favors to Rumi. His life provides real evidence of the Truth. At the same time as he spoke to those of his own times in an effective manner, Rumi was even more influential in that he made his voice and breath, which reflected the voice and breath of Prophet Muhammad, peace and blessings be upon him, continue to be heard for centuries after. He spoke with such an enchanting voice that he was able to guide not only his blessed contemporaries, but also people of our time, centuries removed from his physical existence. God bestowed upon him this important duty. For this purpose, God blessed him with impeccable inner and outer qualities so that he would prove successful in this undertaking. His heart was full of the Divine light. As such, his essence is marked by his wisdom, which shines like a light reflected through a precious gem. His inner-most self was enveloped with Divine mysteries. His inner eyes were enlightened by this special light.

On this horizon, Jalaladdin Rumi represents the North Star, the heart of the circle of guidance for his time. He embodies the characteristics of the lamp of sainthood, taking its light from that of the truth of the Prophet. Many of God's blessed creatures are instinctively attracted to light; Rumi's light has attracted hundreds of thousands spiritual butterflies; they are drawn to the light. He represents a guide for humanity's quest for the perfection of human qualities. Rumi was a careful exegete of the truths presented in the Qur'an. A fluent interpreter of love and zeal for Prophet Muhammad, Rumi was able to use a mysterious language to guide others to a love of God. Those who enter his sphere are able to reach an ultimate sense or feeling in the presence of God. Those who examine the Qur'an by his guideposts underwent changes (and continue to undergo changes) similar to those witnessed by the people who lived in the era of the Prophet himself, peace and blessings be upon him. When the verses of the Qur'an were interpreted by Rumi's closest associates, all hearts benefited from the illumination provided by his wisdom; it was as if all of heaven's mysteries were opened by his wholehearted recitation of that one word-God.

Rumi's love for God was a fiery one, with a constant moaning and longing for the mysteries of God. He experienced a love and passion both in his solitary asceticism and his activities in the community. It was in his solitariness that he became most open to the truest union with God, and it was in such cases of separation from all things except God that he became like a ball of fire. And while such a sense of burning would prove difficult for many to bear, Rumi never showed any signs of discontent. Rather, such a burning was considered a requirement for passion, and refraining from complaint was seen to be in the tradition of loyalty. For Rumi, those who profess a love of God must necessarily accompany their statement of "I love" with a sense of furious burning-this is the price one must willingly pay for being close or in union with God. Additionally, one must engage in behavior that is to a large extent ascetic, such as moderated eating, drinking, sleeping, and a constant awareness and orientation toward God in one's speech, and one must inevitably experience bewilderment when endowed with God's bounties.

Rumi cannot understand how a lover can sleep in an immoderate way, as it takes away from the time that can be shared with the Beloved. For him, excessive sleep is offensive to the Beloved. As God instructed David, saying, "O David, those who indulge in sleep without contemplating Me and then claim to be in love are liars" so too did Rumi state; "When the darkness falls, lovers become intense." Rumi continually recommended this not only in words, but also in his actions.

The following quotation from his Divan-i Kabir best represents several droplets from the ocean of his feelings and excitement, erupting like a volcano:

> *I am like Majnun[1] in my poor heart, which is without limbs, because I have no strength to contest the love of God. Every day and night I continue in my efforts to free myself from the bounds of the chain of love; a chain which keeps me imprisoned. When the dream of the Beloved begins I find myself in blood. Because I am not fully conscious, I am afraid in that I may paint Him with the blood of my heart. In fact, You, O Beloved, must ask the fairies; they know how I have burned through the night. Everyone has gone to sleep. But I, the one who has given his heart to You, do not know sleep like them. Throughout the night, my eyes look at the sky, counting the stars. His love so profoundly took my sleep that I do not really believe it will ever come back.*

If the spirit of the anthology of Rumi's poems, which are the essence of love, passion, divine presence, and excitement, were to be extracted, what would exude are the cries of love, longing, and hope. Throughout his life Rumi expressed love, and in turn, he believed he was beloved because of this. Accordingly, he spoke of his love and relationship with Him. When he did so, he was not alone-he took along with him many blessed individuals who were his audience. He thought that his offering, cup by cup, the drinks presented to him on the heavenly table to others who were in his circle of light to be a sign of loyalty.

Thus, the following quotation represents the ambiguous chanting that is reflected in his heavenly travels:

> *The Buraq[2] of love has taken my mind as well as my heart, do not ask me where. I have reached such a realm that there is no moon, nor day. I have reached a world where the world is no longer the world.*

---

1  *Majnun* is a legendary personality of love found in Islamic literature.
2  *Buraq* is the name of the mount which carried Prophet Muhammad during his Ascension.

This spiritual journey of Rumi was an ascension in the shadow of the Ascension of the Prophet, which is described by Sulayman Chalabi (the author of the *Mawlid* which is recited in the commemoration of the birth of the Prophet) in these words: "There was no space, no Earth, and no heavens." What his soul heard and watched was a special reflection of His courtesy, which cannot be seen by the eyes, cannot be heard by the ears, and cannot be comprehended by one's mind or thought. Such reflections are not attainable by all. Rumi spiritually ascended and saw, tasted, and knew all that was possible for a mortal being. Those who do not see cannot know. Those who do not taste cannot feel. Those who are capable of feeling in this manner generally do not divulge the secrets that they have attained. And those who do reveal these secrets often find them to be above the level of the comprehension of most people. As the famous Turkish poet Sheikh Galib said, "The Beloved's candle has such a wonderful light, its light does not fit into the lamp glass of Heaven."

The love, relationship, and warmth toward all creation as expressed by Rumi is a projection of a deeply-rooted divine love. Rumi, whose nature was intoxicated by the cup of love, embraced all of creation with a projection of that love. He was involved in a dialogue with every creature, and all of these were a result of nothing but his deep love of God and his relationship with the Beloved.

It is not my intention to stir the waters that comprise the lives of such remarkable and pure personalities with debates and questions that ultimately will only agitate and obscure. However, one must wonder whether Rumi opened the horizon of Shams or whether Shams took Rumi to the world of the unseen. Who took whom to the realty of realities-the peak of love and joy? Who directed whom to the real Besought and the real Beloved? Answering these questions is beyond the capacity of most ordinary people. One can say, at least, the following: During this period of time, two skillful and acute spirits came together, like two oceans merging into one another. By sharing the Divine bounties and gifts received from their Lord, they both reached peaks that most peo-

ple would not be able to reach easily on their own accord. Through
their spiritual cooperation, they established camps on the peaks of
knowledge, love, compassion, and joy for God. As much as they
enlightened those of their own age, they also influenced all centuries to follow; an effect that is still present today. The spring of
sweet water which they represent continues to nourish the thirsty.
They have been continuously remembered over the centuries for
their beautiful contributions to countless lives. Here it is important
to note that Rumi was informed by numerous sources in the flow
of ideas, including his father, the great master of scholars. During
his journey, he seemed to leave many of his contemporaries behind-
his love and compassion flowed like the waters of the world's
oceans; so much so that while continuing to live physically among
humans, he managed to become ever closer to God. It seems he
never elevated himself above others except through his writings,
both during his life and after his entering the life of eternity; he
provides a star of guidance that echoes the spiritual life of the
Prophet of Islam. Accordingly, he is among the few people who
have exerted a great influence through both space and time.

Rumi, the Master, was not a pupil, a dervish, a representative,
or master as is known amongst traditional Sufis. He developed a
new method that was colored with revivalism and personal independent reasoning by taking the Qur'an, the Sunna, and Islamic
piety as his points of reference. With a new voice and breath, he
successfully brought both those of his generation and those of
times to follow to a new divine table. As far as his relationship with
God is concerned, he was a man of love and passion. As for those
who turn to him for the sake of God, he represents a compassionate bearer of God's divine cup of love. Yes, as the rains of mercy fall
forth from the clouds of the sky, if the collections of his poems were
to be wrung out, God's love and the love of His Messenger would
gush forth in showers. His Masnavi, exuberant with his spirit, a
book which is in part didactic and was put in the form of a book
by his disciple Husamaddin Chalabi, represents his largest, most
monumental treatise. While it stems from his involvement with the

floods of a high level love and passion, it was presented in smaller waves so that their essence might be understood by a larger part of humanity who did not share the same capacity. His other work, Divan-i Kabir, is both informed by and presented in this higher level of love and passion and better represents his own abilities.

In the Masnavi, feelings and thoughts are put in such a way that they do not confuse our intelligence and in such a style that it does not surpass our understanding. As for the Divan-i Kabir, everything is like an erupting volcano. Its meaning is not easily understood by most. A careful investigation will show that this great book of Rumi's thought will explain such concepts as *baqa billah maallah* (to live by God with God) and *fana fillah* (annihilation in God) in the context of a larger understanding of the world of the unseen. Those who are capable of realizing this excitement in Rumi's Divan will find themselves in extreme bewilderment before a flood of love and ecstasy that is comparable to an erupting volcano. In these poems of the master, which are not easily accessible for most people, the limits of reason are surpassed, the meanings of the poems are elevated above the norms for humanity, and the eternal nature of the unseen world shadows the ephemeral colors and forms of what one encounters in their physical being.

Jalaladdin Rumi was nourished by the fruit of numerous sources of ideas, including religious seminaries, Sufi lodges, and Sufi hermitages associated with strict Sufi asceticism. Rumi attained an understanding of the Ultimate Reality. He cultivated the heavenly through his own methods. Eventually, he became a central star, the North Star, in the sky which houses sainthood. He was like a bright moon that rotates on its own axis. He was a hero who reached the places where he should have reached and stopped where he should have stopped. He read carefully what he saw and evaluated well what he felt. He never displayed or participated in any improper behavior during his journey to God. Even though the numbers were vast, Rumi never lost any of the bountiful gifts he received from the world of the unseen, not even to the weight of an atom. Like many of his predecessors, he voiced these divine bounties through his poetry in an impressive manner. He often voiced his love and excitement in seemingly magic words which resembled the finest of precious gems. Within the vagueness of the poetry, he mastered the art of explaining his ambiguous statements in ways that opened their meaning to friends, but remained obscured to outsiders.

These statements which were at times both clear and ambiguous are the voice and breath of his own horizon-he was not acquainted with other pens or the wells of ink which supplied them. Although one can find a few foreign words or works falsely attributed to him, Rumi's anthology represents a warmth, the music of his own heart, a music which brings all who hear it under its influence with a captivating control.

Rumi possessed a very delicate disposition, often appearing more compassionate than a mother to her child. In short, he was an exceptional personality, particularly in his projection of the spirit of God's Messenger in his own time. This is illustrated in his collected works, including Masnavi, Divan-i Kabir, some collected letters associated with familial relations, and his special behavior with friends. Those who witnessed this were greatly excited to see the perfect heir of the Prophet and would say with great humility and respect, *"This is a grace from God. He gives it to whom He wants"* (Maeda 5:54).

Rumi was a man of genuine sincerity and loyalty. He lived by what he felt in his heart as long as it did not contradict the teachings and laws of religion. While making his faith the focus of his life, while showing the others the way of life, while blowing into the *nay*, while dancing like a butterfly, his heart was burning with love and longing; it had always ached and moaned like the unwavering, steady *nay*. Those who were not aching could not understand him. Those who were rude and tactless could not feel what he felt. He said, "I want a heart which is split, part by part, because of the pain of separation from God, so that I might explain my longing and complaint to it." Saying this, he searched for friends who had similar longings and complaints.

# THE PERCEPTION OF HUMAN IN RUMI

## Ramazan Altıntaş

One of the core issues which Sufis have been looking at is the question of "What is human?" as humankind has a unique position in the entire universe. Rumi's perception of human is, in fact, one of the richest and most comprehensive perspectives among all others. For Rumi, human is like an index for the whole universe. He believes that human is a macrocosm though they may appear to be a microcosm in their form as they are the recipient of God's Attributes.

The word *insan* in Arabic is a non-gendered, non-specific pronoun which refers to humankind in general, but also, in many instances, to any person—someone or anyone, in other words. This word, *insan,* is etymologically a compound made up of the terms *uns* and *nasy.* *Uns,* contrary to alienation, denotes proximity, fondness, love and interest,[1] expounding the person's ease in establishing relations and communication with their own kind as well as their Creator. *Nasy,* on the other hand, is the opposite of awareness of that which has been bestowed, meaning ignorance, forgetting after learning, not understanding, or falling into error;[2] in addition to emphasizing human's predisposition towards concealing the "first covenant,"[3] or the like-

---

[1]  Isfahani, Ragib, *Al-Mufradat fi Garibi'l-Qur'an,* Istanbul, 1986:34; al-Askari, Abu Hilal, *Al-Furuqu'l-Lugawiyya*, Qum, 1974:227.

[2]  Isfahani, ibid, 1986:748; al-Askari, ibid, 1974:227.

[3]  See the Noble Qur'an, A'raf 7/172: "And remember when your Lord brought forth from the children of Adam, from their reins, their seed and made them testify of themselves, (saying): 'Am I not your Lord?' They said: 'Yes, assuredly. We testify!' That was lest you should say at the Day of Resurrection: 'Of this we were unaware'."

lihood of human's rebelling against the Creator, the word also draws attention to a key subject of psychology, namely human beings' inherently weak memory and forgetfulness. The foregoing definition, comprising both the meanings connected with the term *insan,* or human being, concurs with Rumi's own definition of human as the meeting point of sublimity and sordidness, intellect and lust[4]—the most precious of beings, yet one full of innate problems. In order to truly comprehend the nature of human, Rumi advises seekers to resort to the Qur'an and refer to the clear verse:[5] *Surely We have created human of the best stature as the perfect pattern of creation* (Tin 95:4).

As amplified by the verse, it is human, amid the whole of creation, which stands as the best. The concept of "the best stature as the perfect pattern of creation" mentioned in the verse, encompasses all intrinsic beauties, physical or spiritual, from humankind's visible form to their intellectual maturity, endowed as it is with the exceptional capability to recognize and distinguish the signs and indications of reality, not to mention their moral beauty, entrenched with a natural inclination towards gradual development and maturity.[6] Rather than gaining visibility solely through the formal exterior, the true beauty of human comes to the surface through their feelings and spirituality. Thus, by virtue of highlighting the fourth verse of the Qur'an chapter named *Tin,* Rumi effectively draws attention to both the outward and inward beauties of human, for among all creations, human's form and nature is the most exquisite. "Human with his general form and nature," says Rumi, "is greater than the *Divine Throne,* and exceeds the perimeter of thought."[7] It is humankind that is the most polished and perfect mirror to God among all other manifestations of God's Attributes and Names in the universe. Thus, through a synthesis of both physics and metaphysics, Rumi emphasizes the sublimity of humankind for they car-

---

4    Rumi, *Masnavi*, Istanbul, 2004, Vol. IV, 128.

5    Rumi, ibid., Vol. VI, 87.

6    Elmalılı, Muhammed Hamdi Yazır, *Hak Dini Kur'an Dili*, Istanbul, Vol. VIII, 1979:5936.

7    Rumi, ibid., Vol. VI, 87.

ry "an essence from the Transcendent," a manifestation of God, which is the very determinant of their overall value.

Rumi also refers to the following declaration in the Qur'an:

> It is He Who makes all things most excellent which He creates; and He began the creation of humankind from clay. Then He made his seed from an extract of despised water. Then He fashioned him and breathed into him His spirit; and He appointed for you hearing, sight and hearts. Small thanks you give! (Sajda 32:7-9)

These lines essentially establish the fundamental parameters of Islamic aesthetics, of which one aspect is the aesthetic proof for the Existence and Oneness of God, the argument for which is as follows: Human must not linger on nor contend with outward beauty; rather, they must use it as a steppingstone to find a way to the Absolute Beautiful. For it is God Who has bestowed beauty to creation, each carrying an appropriate beauty.[8] Thus, such aesthetic and artistic yearnings in human are natural, corroborated by human's privileged possession in regards to the Divine Breath: *When I have shaped him and breathed My spirit into him…* (Hijr 15:29) means precisely that.[9] Thus, while making each human unique, God has also endowed humankind with some of His attributes, a metaphor elucidated by Rumi as such: "God has created our temperaments and morals according to His Own; hence our attributes are a pattern of His."[10] Rumi, evidently abiding by the gnostic tradition, also alludes to the narration that,[11] "God created Adam in His Own image."[12] The image must obviously be taken in the spiritual sense and not the physical. So, for instance, as God is munificent, we should be generous; as He is a forgiver, so should we be; and so on. Clearly, the

---

8  See the Noble Qur'an, Baqara 2:138 "We take our color from God; and who is better than God at coloring? It is God Who we worship."

9  Rumi, *Masnavi*, Vol. IV, 251.

10  Rumi, ibid., Vol. IV, 106.

11  Rumi, ibid., Vol. IV, 111.

12  Bukhari, *Anbiya*, I; Abu Dawud, *Sunna*, 16.

examples of our reflecting the manifestations of the Creator can be multiplied. The universe is the collection of the manifestations of God's Attributes and Names, and those manifestations are focused on humankind. Individual members of humanity reflect a limited number of manifestations of the light of His Existence. In enunciating this issue, Rumi adds that, "Just how the Creator wants to be exalted and thanked, so does human."[13] For human, according to Rumi, is the recipient of God's attributes. This demonstrates the high value accorded to humankind.

Owing to God's rendition of human in His image, as knowledgeable and wise, human may occasionally witness the matchless beauty and theophany of God, in flashes, through the astrolabe of their own existence—a beauty which can never be detached from this mirror.[14] For human, the road to attaining this beauty lies in wiping the mirror of the heart with repentance and polishing it with the remembrance of God. For this reason, Rumi's entire endeavor is to emphatically stress the fact that by virtue of drawing attention to the relationship between God and humankind, humanity's greatest virtue, ethically speaking, will be to attain the model of *Insan-i Kamil,* or Universal Human. Additionally, by giving mention to the aphorism of Caliph Ali which states that, "Human seems like a small universe but, in fact, he is the greatest universe,"[15] Rumi elaborates the attributes that grant superiority to humankind over other creations through the application of analogy.

In effect, the purpose is to identify the main points of demarcation between the sublime and the base, between the angelic and animalistic attributes of human. Within this context, Rumi categorizes beings, as regards their natural creation, into three. The children of Adam, or humankind, in terms of their creation, possess both angelic and animalistic attributes. Thus, as observed by Rumi, human has a power of anger and lust in addition to their power of

---

13  Rumi, *Masnavi*, Vol. IV, 106.

14  Rumi, *Fihi Ma Fihi*, Istanbul, 1985:17-18.

15  Rumi, *Masnavi*, Vol. IV, 57.

intellect and knowledge. A human being, in whom the power of lust has become dominant over the intellect, would be prone to vices such as injustice; conversely, if the latter has overpowered the former, they would exhibit virtuous behavior such as chastity, courage and justice.[16]

Applying this model, Rumi defines human[17] by first acknowledging that a portion of human beings have devoted their entire lives to God. These, in a way, have joined the process of *angelization*, like Jesus Christ, by casting practical faith and Islam—submission to One God—into their daily lives. These people, in the words of Rumi, are "outwardly human, but inward *a la* Gabriel." Indeed, they have been liberated entirely from anger, backbiting, lust and desire. Fasting, for instance, symbolizes this perfectly, as a fasting Muslim, by abstaining throughout the day from eating, drinking and the lower desires of the self in general, brings to the fore his angelic side.

According to Rumi, another portion of human beings have, on the other hand, joined the herd of donkeys. They have virtually become anger itself, embalmed from head to toe in lust. Akin to the rest of creation, they eat, drink and fulfill their animalistic desires just for the sake of appeasing their physical needs. As their relation with God is severed, they possess none of the angelic or spiritual attributes, as Rumi relates his observations to the verse,[18] *O ye who believe! Respond to God and to the Messenger when the Messenger calls you (in the Name of God) to that which gives you life!* (Anfal 8:24) Thus it is critical for one not to become detached from the resuscitating revelation, as doing so will push him into the throes of depression. For this reason, Rumi lights the correct path for the perplexed to take by expounding, "Take your mind that is in the service of religion as a guide."[19]

---

16  Rumi, ibid., Vol. IV, 128.
17  See Rumi, ibid., Vol. IV, 128-129.
18  See Rumi, ibid., Vol. IV, 124-125.
19  Rumi, ibid., Vol. IV, 53.

Humankind, according to Rumi, is an enormous universe bearing all, and out of all creations, it is they who possess the most, and best, of God's innumerable and exalted attributes. All of God's Names which have given existence to the whole universe are manifested in humanity in direct proportion to their obeying God and His Messenger. They have been created capable of both good and bad, that they might use their will to succeed in the trials of life. Thus, with the free will they possess, humankind is instructed to utilize their capabilities for the service of good. Rumi explicitly repudiates the incongruence of the materialist notion of human by pronouncing, "If human was considered only as a physical entity, Ahmad (i.e., Prophet Muhammad, upon whom be peace) and Abu Jahl would have been level."[20] As described by matchless prose and poetry of Rumi, human contains such immense love, greed, lust and sorrow that even if they were to own hundreds and thousands of universes, they would still find peace elusive. For all these pleasures and desires are analogous to a ladder whose steps are made to walk over and climb, not as a surface on which to rest.[21] Therefore, human must not, in vain, search for peace and tranquility upon each step, but in the ultimate faith in God to which they must ascend.

---

20   Rumi, ibid., Vol. I, 82.
21   For more information see Rumi, *Fihi Ma Fihi*, Istanbul, 1985:99.

# THE MEMETIC COUNSELING OF MASNAVI: THE ARTLESS ART OF JALALADDIN RUMI

Seema Arif

L ife in the postmodern world has not been an easy challenge for humanity, where there are teddy bears instead of live pets in the arms of small children, and hands wrapped around computer joysticks instead of the fingers of a young sibling. What has been cracked is the human bond with life and with nature, and what has been strengthened is the contact with material objects. It is an automated world germinated by the idea of self-sustenance and self-growth at the cost of virtually everything else. However, the question which the hi-tech world puts before us is not easy to answer. Whereas, on the one hand, it challenges the traditional belief system, it also asks us to know the true nature of the universe; to satiate the spirit of inquiry and describe where we really came from; to define the noble purpose of life; to free ourselves from nonsensical guilt mechanisms; to teach in order to invigorate our inner selves and outer-strength mechanism; and to equip ourselves with the ultimate tool for self-fulfillment and happiness.

As human knowledge advances, the human intellect is rapidly shifting towards godless ideas of existence, morality and humanism, where religion is referred to as "a virus of the mind," a concept of antiquity, or a creation of the prehistoric mind requiring rethinking and re-evaluation. The concept of the evolution of thinking is one key tool by which such proponents reach their objective. They find human thinking to be a gradually evolved process by which certain conceptualization and problem-solving abilities emerged as human beings consciously adapted to face the new challenges of life.

Within such a framework, there is no room for the creation of man as an intelligent being with knowledge awarded to him to allow him to survive as God's vicegerent on earth. Instead, successful patterns of thought and behavior are supposed to be autonomously transmitted not only to the next generation, but also to rapidly transfuse and inspire the minds and behaviors of the current generation.

This manner of replication of ideas is called "memetics," and the methodology of replication is essentially "imitation." A "meme" attempts to completely, logically, and scientifically explain the universe around us, and to define a purpose for us. It can be any idea, fashion, fad, or some scientific theory which captures the attention of human mind for the time being, as reflected in contemporary music such as Bon Jovi's album, "Have A Nice Day," which clearly illustrates how we easily fall into the trap of blind imitation without ever giving any serious thought to our behaviors or attitudes.

Hence, the essential question regarding this notion of memetic transfer is whether it is the temporary assurance or permanent solution of a human enigma. We acknowledge that people tend towards choosing quick fixes rather than finding permanent solutions to ethical dilemmas, which leads to the corruption of society and the distribution of pain rather than happiness—isolating individuals rather than bringing them together. Why? Why we are getting more and more sick, depressed or aggressive day-by-day? What is missing or left far behind?

A voice from past reminds us. Yet in this world powered by self-centered deism and theism, the cry for life remains unheard, or hushed down. There are wild guitars and sensuous drumbeats to dance the life out of you, but no sweet reed to harmonize you to the tune of "life." We are told that such darkened times have occurred before, when Mongol terror reigned over the world. Mankind was suffering, skeptical, lacking trust, jealous, envious and hypocritical, as human hearts blackened and countless souls were rapidly sold to the devil. At such a time, a man arose with the wisdom of the ages whispering into the ears of humanity the song of life, the cause of eternity, and the proof of existence. It was none other than our beloved

Mawlana Jalaladdin Rumi—the ultimate sage, counselor, and healer of bleeding hearts and wounded souls.

A counselor is a guide who provides an intervention and inspires
us to seek solutions to our problems. These solutions may not be
provided within the paradigm of the stereotypical behaviors followed
in society, nor discussed in textbooks in classic or exemplary ways.
However, holding this matter as being critically important in deter-
mining the intellectual health and survival of a society, Rumi, in his
*Masnavi*, addressed the particular issue of the thoughtful following
of a tradition versus the aimless imitation of certain stereotypes in
behavior and conduct.

Life is not merely sick—it is on death bed. Is there any cure?
Can some potion revive and rejuvenate the spirit of life? Mawlana
Jalaladdin Rumi ensures us that. Yes, there is. It is love, the communication with truth. How such a communication ever be truly
possible? Can we "see" ourselves in the truest of lights, without any
shade of personal desire? And here comes the greatest gift of Rumi—
the mirror.

Rumi's command is to put the mirror of love in front of humanity and see whether the reflection is that of a beauty or a beast. What
will the mirror tell us? It will show powder-laden, cosmetically lifted faces, or the doubtful, skeptical, misery-laden hearts of our times,
hearts weak and insecure, crying under weight of life. There is doom
and there is darkness. Is there any light—any knowledge? Can we
find any woe-free heart around us?

If there is a mirror for this world, it has rusted too much to
properly reflect the pain and suffering of the poor, the helpless and
the downtrodden. It mirrors one thing and reflects something else.
The call for peace and unity is the slogan of globalism, but its flag
is stained by bloodshed and the massacre of innocent souls. Why is
there such a veil? What is it trying to hide? Rumi answers: The veil
is human ignorance rooted in the deep insecurity challenging self-
esteem and self-worth, and thus, the existence of individual life.
The ignorance is a mask which is put over by the selfishness of the
lower-self as it wails over its own inefficiency. It is the incapacity of
one to see.

HOW DO WE SEE OURSELVES?

The great Sufi poet Syed Buleh Shah, from Punjab, exclaims in a frenzy:

*Buleha[1]! I wonder who I am!*

He seeks countless explanations as to whether he is of a particular religion—a Hindu, a Muslim, a Christian or a Sikh—and whether he is good or evil, a pious soul or a devil. Many of us ask such questions about ourselves, and we reach different answers. Dr. Deepak Chopra writes about the ancient beliefs of various religions culminating in a single realization:

*There is likeness of man's exterior to all other men...*
*There is likeness of man's interior with God ...*

A Hadith is often quoted in Muslim Sufi texts, especially that of Ibn-Arabi:

*Man 'arafa nafsahu faqad 'arafa Rabbahu.*

It may be translated as:

*A better understanding of the human "self"*
*leads to a proper concept of God.*

No doubt, modern human thinking about the self has been greatly influenced by Karl Marx's notion of man as the "zoon politikon," or social animal. It was Karl Marx who argued that "it is not the consciousness of men that determines their existence, but on

Deception  Cruelty  Foe  Death  Fear  Thorn  Mean  Unjust  Venom  Snake Bite  Antidote  Flower  Generous  Hope  Gift  Life  Justice  Friend  Fair

---

[1] Buleha is the name of the poet, who is addressing to himself here.

the contrary, their social existence determines their consciousness." But it is Rumi who guides us as he states that when social reality dominates individual reality, conformity and imitation will be on rise and this memetic business will flourish, because the inner eye will be put to sleep, the compass will be shadowed, and "the mirror will be rusted":

> *Dost thou know why the mirror (of thy soul) reflects nothing?*
> *It is because the rust is not cleared from its face.*

Unfortunately, post-modern materialist thinking has been more Platonic, interested in studying the static view of "being," rather than evolving the Aristotelian sense of "becoming," or Rumi's notion of "*sama*"—not simply revolving, but evolving an attempt to reach "supra-conscious."

Instead, leaving conscious reality aside, modern social science even perceives "Darwinian Evolution" as the subjective reality of matter, addressing its material worth only. It is an anti-clock movement screwing human consciousness into a pit of darkness and evil instead of lifting it to holy ascension. In the dark, all creepy, crawling realities migrate onto the surface of life and begin their savage rule and command over our existence. It is this single-eyed vision that is unable to "see" or sense natural beauty; and so, only a carefully masked and crafted cosmetic sense of beauty is cultivated. The greatest loss is that of the sense of beauty, because with it, humanity loses its sense of purity, and of harmony with nature. And as material bounty corrupts morality, social affluence jeopardizes it further as sharing is replaced by possessing; and friendly competition turns into black envy, mutating into enmity and bloody rivalry.

The inability to deal with diversity and the changing perspective of reality creates illusions and faulty percepts, just as moving a torch rapidly in the shape of a circle gives the impression that there is a circle of fire. Speaking of squinted vision in "The Shopkeeper and the Parrot,"[2] Rumi warns that faulty vision creates doubts as one sees many in one.

---

[2]   *Masnavi*, Vol I, 2nd Story.

## UNVEILING

It is a basic human tendency to view things in parts, and thus individuals fall into holes, and ultimately into the eternal pitfall of ignorance. We perceive various phenomena occurring in nature using a monocle by which we can only observe one track of cause and effect, whereas in actuality, things are moving on multiple tracks. There is always a counter-track to restore balance in nature, just as there is a centripetal force to counter centrifugal force.

> He has let loose the two seas meeting together. Between them is a barrier which none of them can transgress. (Rahman 55:19-20)

While explaining the 19<sup>th</sup> verse of Surah Rahman of the Qur'an, Rumi clearly extrapolates how, in the same flow of life, various elements have certain distinct and contradictory effects, and these sharp opposites still ascertain a quality of unity such that it is hard to identify the isolation point existing between them. He further explains it by using the analogy of a snake bite: in various situations, the utility and thus the perception of its effect can be quite contrary to each other.

What we have learned here is simply that God has created cause and effect: assigning values to these phenomena is the domain of "axiology," while defining the quality of existence is the sphere of "ontology." So while these are essential human percepts influencing human knowledge and thought processes, they do not, and cannot, influence the process of Divine Laws. This frustration leads towards fatalism, as man tries to isolate himself from the universal reality and truth. This is the greatest injustice that a man can do to himself. So what is so illusory and deceiving, Rumi asks,

*The Self... or all these human percepts about self?*

Through words such as these, Rumi acts as the rescuer of humanity, lifting the veil over imperceptible acts of cognition and clearing the vision. He liberates human consciousness of all doubts by gaining the right knowledge and by shifting our perceptions towards the optimum paradigm for the construction and reconstruction of observed phenomenon. It is the balancing of vision, focusing at the ends of a continuum the external reality, the objective truth and the internal reality, and the subjective truth, which leads towards knowledge of the ultimate truth. He openly declares:

> *Only knowledge of truth and of love and beauty not cosmetically crafted but mirrored by the art of nature embellished by sincerity, trust, belonging, and sacrifice teaches the lesson slowly learned by sickened souls to transform themselves into the master of hearts.*

While doing so, Rumi does not operate through mere skepticism; rather, he digs deeply into the moralism which shapes society's ethics through questioning its utility and application. His careful insights, developed through detailed analysis and synthesis, not only enlighten us about the pitfalls of certain thinking patterns and the faulty behaviors which emerge as a result, but also provide us with the remedy and guidance to correct what is wrong in order to adapt to what is right. In this way, he does not admonish us, in effect, but simply relates the enigmas and paradoxes of life, to strengthen our souls so that we might resist and repel all that is unnatural, impure, and thus, inhuman.

Mawlana Jalaladdin Rumi's "mirror" is a tool gifted to mankind not only to adorn our selves but to beautify our souls in harmony with divine principles, as taught by the Qur'an and practiced to perfection by the Prophet Muhammad (pbuh). We witness the birth of a caring heart and a contemplative soul—a heart that cares for the miseries of others and a soul that broods over personal mistakes rather than self-inflicted miseries, a heart that is not a beggar of mercy or affection from others, but a heart generous enough to share the little "happinesses of life" with others to deliver the ultimate contentment. In short, life needs nurturance and it demands care. We need the knowledge of the "right"—in other words, the consciousness of what is "good" in life. Step-by-step, Rumi leads and teaches us to discover and unveil hypocrisy, to avoid flattery, to be sen-

sible with our tongues, to defeat envy, and ultimately, to free ourselves from the slavery of our lower selves.

The result is a paradigm shift in the purpose of life as it moves
from the notion of "rule over life" to that of "serving one's life." It
is the "new knowledge" of the heart, which reconstructs the experience of existence. It is not limiting consciousness to one source of
knowledge or another. Rather, it involves breaking the limits and
freeing the consciousness from the shackles of the lower self to find
new ways and means of adapting to the universal principles of life.
It consists not in breaking boundaries but in broadening the horizon that one feels when one is set free from the pull of gravity, as
the earthen magic pulls and enters into the mesmerism of flying
through the air and the final bliss and tranquility that one enjoys
when being evacuated into the unlimited boundaries of space. In
this, Rumi becomes the enchanted liberator, divinely blessed, as his
guidance helps us to learn to progress gradually in the cycle of consciousness, emerging naturally during the mega memes or "meme-
plexes" of the "I" and "life." Thus, Masnavi becomes the hermeneu-
tic experience of the Qur'an as it teaches us all about life and also
leads us to determine the relative position of the "I" in context of
"life."

What is psychology? And what does psychological counseling
address? It is simply the reconstruction of human experience. Rumi
deals with it himself, but slowly and gradually, liberating a human
soul from the bounds of ignorance as softly as a rose erupts from
its bud with all its shining color and fragrance. Thus, adopting the
disposition of an adept social scientist, Rumi cleverly maneuvers
through the problems faced in all social spheres.

Modern social sciences try to fix themselves to the story of the
"self" or "society" alone, like the wooden horse which can never experience the ascension or the "Flight with Buraq," rising to the third
dimension and aspiring to speak of the soul and the percepts of metaphysics. Few can tell this tale like Rumi, who has coded the history of Muslim civilization, its thought and beliefs, and the evolution
and devolution of its culture in the *Masnavi*. All analogies used by

him are carefully constructed memes, whose vigilant decoding leads us to an exquisite unveiling of a greater truth. Through this systematic analysis and synthesis, Rumi successfully handles modern discourse techniques. The use of dialectics to reach down to the core of a problem, disclosing it part-by-part until it is obvious to the naked eye and then gradually reconstructing it by assigning it new value with meaning and purpose is the artless art of Rumi. The truth is life itself, where there is no bias nor religious or cultural barrier. Hence, Rumi achieves a universal language which is communicable to people of all ages across time.

# RUMI RESONATES THROUGH THE AGES
## Michaela M. Özelsel

**M**awlana Jalaladdin Rumi's tomb is not merely a splendid monument; it also has an atmosphere that escorts us to our inner world, to the heart, to God, Who says in the Qur'an: *We are nearer to him than his jugular vein* (Qaf 50:16). This tomb is a place of peace, a place of the timeless holiness that wafts around the visitors like a breeze from a sphere beyond time.

All this is real; yet Rumi himself implored us not to search for him in his grave. He is still present with us, a living presence, and his being transcends his grave. He speaks to people of all ages, all races, all nations, and all walks of life, and says: *"Come, come, come again, whoever you may be..."* His message is God's message to mankind, reaching us pure and clear through the "empty flute" which Rumi has become. When he describes the different levels of understanding of the Holy Qur'an, he is describing his own work at the same time. As we develop mentally we can better understand Rumi's messages which have been sent to us across the borders of space and time.

His parables are taken from daily life; no matter how trivial they may seem, dealing with chickpeas, *halva*,[1] the wind, the ocean, or the nose ring of a dancing bear ... They are distinct symbols pointing to things that are incomprehensible and transcendental. Rumi is a "translator" of the divine message.

The works of Rumi, in particular the simply formulated *Fihi ma Fihi*, have always granted me access to deeper and deeper levels of the Qur'an. Surely the Holy Qur'an is infinitely complex, but for

---

[1]  A Turkish dessert prepared in many varieties with sesame oil, various cereals, and syrup or honey.

me, Rumi's works are infinitely complex as well. For 10 years I have been reading *Fihi ma Fihi*, yet I have still not come to the end. Each and every time I reach new and deeper levels of understanding, and every single discovery I make there also takes me to a new level of understanding the Qur'an.

But all this, I am sure, is more than my "own personal experience." In this respect I think that I can speak for all Muslims who sympathize with the Sufi way of thinking. But, if we assume that Rumi speaks to every man and woman, then what about the rest of mankind? Where do we find his message for those non-Muslims, non-Christians, non-Jews, and for those other people who do not believe in the existence of the Beyond? What are those presents, which God has provided for the creatures of his creation, "wrapped up" in? One such "wrapping" is psychotherapy.

## THE DOOR OF HOPE

I'm a psychologist from the West, a psychotherapist educated in the USA and in Germany in the most advanced methods the Western industrialized nations have developed.

As long as relatively simple mental disorders, like phobias are concerned, the methods I was taught in university are quite effective and helpful for my patients. But what kind of therapy is efficient to deal with serious existential crises? What can I do if a patient is so desperate that he thinks he is no longer able to live? What if someone has lost everything that meant something to him by "a stroke of fate"? What if someone has lost his innermost structure, his self-esteem, or even his "manhood" because he has been humiliated or tortured? Incidents like these mark the limits of classic Western methods. (In recent decades, in addition to these "classic" methods, some new methods arose, for example some approaches of existential or transpersonal therapy. These rely to a great extent on the spiritual knowledge of the Near and the Far East. They help us and can also serve as a framework for the works of Rumi.) Rumi encourages us to cross the bounds of despair and shows us the door of hope. Actually, he shows us new ways to make use of Islamic virtues like trust, hope, steadfastness, and patience and thereby find a cure. He helps us to become greater than our pain and to reach higher levels within ourselves. He helps us to transform our deep pain into mental development, as he himself has taken the same way before us. How severely he must have suffered when he lost his beloved teacher Shamsaddin, not only once, but twice.

Day by day people who suffer from pain and look for help come and see us, psychotherapists. Rumi shows us that pain may end up in maturation and mental development as long as it is handled appropriately. That is, we should not protest in times of pain (because this comes from God, too), but rather accept it in a very conscious way. Otherwise, we might get caught up in one of those traps that prevent mental development: self-pity (Why me?), hatred for other people ("If he hadn't acted in such a way, things would have gone better..."), or the rationalization of the fox in Aesop's fable, *sour grapes*. In this way, one devaluates what they cannot have, something that they would really like to have had and thus cheats their own soul.

To walk right into a trap like this is only human. It is very tempting, because it reduces the pain for a short time. But at the same time it also prevents us from maturing spiritually. Rumi in his grief over Shams managed to avoid these traps. Instead he transformed himself. By saying, "I was raw, I became cooked, I was burnt" he summarized his path of reaching annihilation in God *(fana)* and subsistence with God *(baqa)*. He took this way before us and he left much advice for us to enable us to follow in his footsteps. He said for example:

> Sorrows are a divine grace. As long as people feel good they forget about the Creator. But in times of sorrow and pain they think of Him. When the sorrow comes, the veil of forgetfulness is torn apart and the sufferer accepts God and wails: "O God, O You Who are Merciful!" He is being cured, but soon the veil of forgetfulness falls down again, and he says: "Where is God? I cannot find Him. I do not see Him. What shall I look for?"

Why were you able to find him when you suffered but cannot find him now? So now you see that as you suffer, God makes you think of Him sending you sorrow and pain.[2]

"To consume worries" means to empty oneself. After such an emptying joy appears, a kind of joy that knows no sorrow—a rose without thorns, a wine that does not bring headaches.[3]

It is the sorrow that guides us. As long as there is no sorrow, no passion, or no yearning love in a work we will not strive for it. Without sorrow it remains out of our reach.[4]

But who are we anyway? Freud, the "father" of Western psychology, provides us with a rather negative, resigned image of human beings. Not so Rumi. He points to all the opportunities we have and which may be activated under certain circumstances—if only we overcome our ego (*nafs*). He shows us the meaning of the following verses by means of his wonderfully concise metaphor, the "angel's wings" and the "donkey's tail." *And the soul and Him Who made it perfect, then He inspired it to understand what is right and wrong for it; he will indeed be successful who purifies it, and he will indeed fail who corrupts it.* (Shams 91:7-10) Humans are creatures equipped with the wings of angels that are tied up with the tail of a donkey. The wings pull us up, but the tail pulls us back down. Poor human beings are torn in between.[5]

This picture has helped so many of my patients who have been trapped between insight (angel's wings) and desires (donkey's tail), patients who are suffering from various addictions. The angel's wings, for instance, tell them: "Do not smoke, do not drink, do not eat too much!" while the donkey's tail whispers: "One more drink will do no harm, cigarettes are not that dangerous, only a little more *halva*..." If I explain this metaphor to them, they start laughing. At once they stop feeling humiliated by their own conduct. They draw new hope

---

[2]  *Fihi ma Fihi*, 58, p. 342.

[3]  Ibid., 27, p. 200.

[4]  Ibid., 5, p. 75.

[5]  Ibid., 18, p. 150.

and new courage. Then I encourage them to draw pictures of the angel's wings and the donkey's tail and to pin them on the fridge, the liquor bottle, or the sweets. If they become tempted they look at these pictures and ask themselves: "Which direction do I really want to go? Do I want to go down lower than cattle? (A'raf 7:177) Or do I want to make the most of my potential? In this way the metaphor has helped many people and has not only brought hope, but also humor and new power to a situation that was once desperate.

Another important point with these patients is the shame and the sense of guilt about not having behaved in the right way (to the best of their knowledge) over a long period of time. Often this shame results in resignation: "I have sunk so low, there's no sense in trying harder. I will never escape this misery." But Rumi's parables can change this fatal attitude: Frequently it is the bad that brings about the good. (See: *And it may be that you dislike a thing while it is good for you* [Baqara 2:216] and *Except him who repents and believes and does a good deed; so these are they of whom God changes the evil deeds to good ones* [Furqan 25:70]) Everything a bad person once did by the depravity of thought now becomes a powerful force that improves their thought. So if a sly thief regrets what they have done in the past and becomes a policeman, they will be a better policeman than others who were not thieves.[6]

While traditional psychoanalysis deals with the past and the question "why?", Rumi's approach is a precursor of the latest Western methods, which aim at alterations in the here and now and strive to change the present—and thus the future—without exploring the "why." "Do not say: 'I followed crooked ways,' but choose the straight way, so nothing will stay crooked... If you become straight all crookedness will disappear. Watch out, do not lose hope!"[7] These are exactly the messages that are behind the most advanced therapeutic methods of today.

---

6    Ibid., 32, p. 225.
7    Ibid., 1, p. 60.

Nevertheless, there will always be things in life that we cannot alter no matter how hard we try. If fate is unkind to us sometimes we can see no way out. If we are Muslims, then we know: "If the ego *(nafs)* urges us to complain, do not complain; rather give thanks instead." But how can we convey this insight to non-Muslims? Once again Rumi guides the way:

> This is the way of the dervishes. When the mind wants to complain, do the opposite—give thanks. Exaggerate the matter to such a degree that you find within yourself a love of what repels you. Pretending thankfulness is a way of seeking the love of God.[8]

My work with patients has proven that the concept of "pretending thankfulness," which may appear somewhat strange, in practice brings about very interesting results. Thanks to this concept, patients who have had to cope with severe grief realize where there still are attachments and to what extent they are really ready to let things go and to accept the new situation that is the result of their losses. *Surely God is with the patient* (Baqara 2:153). Enduring grief patiently may foster mental development and inner cleansing. Rumi illustrates this fact with an example that sounds strange in post-feminist times: He suggests to us a married life in the "way of Muhammad" as opposed to that in the "way of Jesus": "(One of the ways) is to get married and to endure the tyranny of women, to listen to their arguments and to remain patient, to tolerate them, not to get angry about them, and to refine oneself... Their rage and aggression will refine your character if you put up with them, but corrupt their own character... If you have understood this, then clean up yourself. ... After that you wish without thinking twice to be patient, to fight, and to suffer, because you see it as a source of benefit."[9]

I think that one can easily replace the word "women" with "men." Here Rumi is showing us the process of purification through consciously enduring sorrow and grief by applying a (drastic) example that the audience of his time (probably mostly men) could under-

---

[8] Ibid., 64, p. 366.
[9] Ibid., 21, p. 162.

stand. The same process and the same method are still valid today, only he might have chosen another metaphor. (The fact that these words cause offense today indicates that Rumi used to "wrap up" eternal truths: He spoke to the people in a way that enabled them to understand him, and he called others to do the same: *"I choose words that suit the understanding and skills of the people. Consider the intelligence of the people as you talk to them."*[10]

In the Western practice there are religious patients or patients of faith who have quite a distorted understanding of belief. They think that every stroke of fate is a punishment from God. Their corresponding feelings of shame and guilt prevent them from dealing with the situation in a constructive way. Rumi, time and again finds therapeutically useful examples to demonstrate us that God tests us with the good and the bad, as He himself assures to us: *We tried them with blessings and misfortunes that they might turn* (A'raf 7:168). Therefore things that seem bad to us may, on the contrary, be seen as a test or a challenge and in the long run be good for us. This range of vision makes it possible to deal with strokes of fate in a constructive way. Consider Rumi's story of the jackal pups: In this story Jesus is asked to leave a safe place because those cubs need quiet and security. So Jesus complains that even the jackal pups are treated better than he and receives the following answer: "The jackal pups have a home, but they do not have a lover who turns them out of the house. The favor of such a One to turn them out and a graceful dress of honor that does not fit everybody He only grants to you alone. So He makes the anonymous place your place and ranks you among His confidants. And that is worth so much more..."[11]

Rumi has taught us not only with his words but also by his deeds, like the whirling ritual (*sama*) and retreat (*chila* or *halwat*); these also can be used for healing. New physiological examinations of the brain have proven that during the *sama* the rotation around the axis of the body combined with a slight inclination of the head

---

[10]  Hadith quoted in *Fihi ma Fihi*, 24, p. 183.

[11]  *Fihi ma Fihi*, 11, p. 103.

to the right induces a so called "kinetic trance." This is an excellent basis for "deleting" old conditioned patterns in the brain and for taking up new, more appropriate knowledge.[12] Besides, this state of consciousness allows us to adjust our biorhythms, the so called ultradian cycles, which can go awry due to stress. Perhaps it is this adjustment process that also forms the basis of shamanic healings.[13] It is for this reason that the *sama* can influence the healing of the body in a positive way through mental-spiritual healing.

While there is no problem trying to understand the fundamentals of the *sama* in the West, a comprehension of the Mawlavi retreat *(matbah chilasi)* is very difficult. It takes so much time that it is not a realistic method of treatment. On the other hand a 40-day retreat *(halwat)* is possible for some patients. (I have done this twice, as well as studying the experiences of other Westerners, including non-Muslims.[14] This method presents us with an enormous therapeutic potential that needs to be further examined in the West.

I have had the opportunity to talk to psychologists and psychiatrists in Turkey as I am being invited frequently by Turkish universities for conferences and conventions. Each invitation gives me a lot of pleasure but sometimes when I talk to my fellow psychologists and psychiatrists there I also feel a bit sad. Many of them just imitate a knowledge of the West which is obsolete even in the West itself. In my opinion this is the saddest thing, because Turkey and the Islamic culture possess the most advanced methods. The heritage of the great therapists of the time of Islamic prosperity, like Ibn Sina (Avicenna), Ibn Rushd (Averroes), Abu Bakr Razi, Al-Farabi, Hasan Suuri, and others still lives on in very specific writings of the Sufi masters. Not only my beloved Rumi, but also Yunus Emre, Hoca Ahmet Yesevi and others provide us with messages that are still significant today. Also the "oriental music therapy" that Güvenç has reintroduced

---

[12]  Winkelmann, 1990.

[13]  Rossi, 1993.

[14]  Özelsel, 1993.

to us today is more appreciated and widespread in the West than it is in the countries of origin.

Over and over, I have received invitations to American conventions; in the United States people are very interested in integrating the therapies from ancient cultures into contemporary Western culture—be it through Rumi's metaphors (this kind of therapy is called "cognitive restructuring") *sama, dhikr, halwat,* or through music therapy. I wish the same will happen in my second home, Turkey, where Rumi emigrated at an early age and produced all of his works.

Who knows how far we will get in matters of healing ourselves or in striving to do something for mankind in general? We cannot know before we try. Trust and hope are our wings, and Rumi is a master in unfolding them. So I would like to end the topic with his concise words: "A bird that tries hard to fly higher and higher will never reach the heaven, but every single moment it will soar from the earth and fly higher than all the other birds."[15]

REFERENCES

- Hz. Mevlana (1988); *Von Allem und vom Einen, Fihi ma Fihi*; München, Diederichs Verlag.
- Özelsel, M., (1993); *40 Tage - Erfahrungsbericht einer traditionellen Derwischklausur*; München. Diederichs.
- Rossi, E.; *Die Psychobiologie der Seele-Körper Heilung*; Essen, Synthesis Verlag.
- Winkelmann, M. (1990); *Shamans, Priests and Witches*; Arizona State University: Anthropological Research Papers No. 44.

---

[15] *Fihi ma Fihi*, 44, p. 284.

# PART II

The Life of Rumi and Mevlevi Sufism

# MAWLANA JALALADDIN MUHAMMAD RUMI

Adnan Karaismailoğlu

Jalaladdin Muhammad, with whom the epithet *Mawlana* (our master) has acquired a unique meaning, was born on the 30$^{th}$ of September, 1207 in Balkh, currently situated in northern Afghanistan. Mawlana Jalaladdin Muhammad is also known to the world simply as Rumi, meaning "from Roman Anatolia" because Anatolia used to be called the "land of Rum (Romans)." Balkh, one of the principal cities of a region holding pivotal importance in the Anatolian tradition, that is to say Khorasan, was occupied, at the time of his birth, by the Khawarzmshahs, and previously by the Seljuks and Ghaznavids. The Guris, beginning from 1198, had briefly occupied the city, prior to the capture of it by the Khawarzmshah in 1206, after which emerged the ensuing Mongolian threat.

Rumi's father, Bahaaddin Muhammad, renowned as *Sultanu'l-Ulama* (the Sultan of Scholars), was from a family prominent in producing eminent scholars and gnostics alike. Despite the fact that the sources mention previous notable figures throughout the family line, it was first and foremost Rumi, then his father, Bahaaddin, and his son, Sultan Walad, who imprinted their marks on history. For a reason unknown, Bahaaddin Muhammad departed Balkh with his family and crowded entourage, either in 1212, 1213 or 1219. In addition to experiencing then-current political dilemmas, he probably also felt indignant towards theologian Fakhraddin Razi (d.1210), whose opinions he criticized, and the ruler Muhammmad of Khawarzmshah, who displayed sympathy towards those very opinions.

## IN SEARCH OF A NEW LAND

Though his wife, Mumina Hatun, his elder son, Alaaddin Muhammad, and Rumi accompanied Bahaaddin in the departing caravan, his daughter, Fatima Hatun, being married, remained in Balkh. The caravan initially visited Nishabur and Baghdad, followed by a pilgrimage to the Hijaz, and then via Damascus concluded their journey in Anatolia. According to Ahmad-i Aflaki, after leaving Damascus, the caravan reached the Anatolian cities of Malatya first, then Erzincan, whereupon they embarked for the proximal Akşehir, their residence for the next four years, eventually settling at Larende (Karaman), where they remained for a further seven years or more.[1] However, another chronicler, Sipahsalar, narrates the journey with a slight difference, so that from the Hijaz, in sequence, they went to Damascus, Erzincan, then Akşehir, staying there throughout the winter, after which they reached Konya in present-day Turkey.[2]

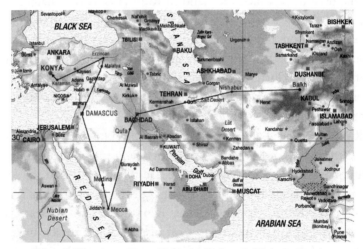

Sultanu'l-Ulama's en route with his family from Balkh in present-day
Afghanistan to Konya in present-day Turkey.

Larende proved to be a stopover of special importance for the family, as it was there, in 1225, that Rumi married Gavhar Hatun, from the same caravan, daughter of Lala Sharafaddin of Samarqand, a marriage which graciously produced Sultan Walad in 1226, and lat-

---

1     Aflaki, *Ariflerin Menkibeleri* (The Glorious Talents and Abilities of the Knowers of God), I, Istanbul, 1986:99-101.

2     Sipahsalar, *Mevlana ve Etrafindakiler* (Mawlana and his Entourage), Istanbul, 1977: 22-23.

er, Alaaddin Chalabi. During this seven-year stay in Larende, both Rumi's mother, Mumina Hatun, and elder brother, Alaaddin Muhammad, passed away and were subsequently buried in the location currently known as *Madar-i Mawlana,* meaning Rumi's Mother.

Taking his family with him, *Sultanu'l-Ulama* Bahaaddin Muhammad migrated to Konya, capital city of the Anatolian Seljuk Turks. By the time of his death, on 23 February, 1231,[3] aged 85 according to the account of Ahmad-i Aflaki, Rumi was 24 years of age.[4]

Thereafter, Rumi was required to assume the position of his erudite and scholarly father. Upon arrival in Konya, Rumi became a disciple of Sheikh Burhanaddin-i Muhakkik-i Tirmidhi, a disciple of Rumi's late father, known as Sayyid-i Sirdan, a devotion lasting seven years. Following his master's recommendation that he should seek further education, Rumi traveled to and briefly stayed in Damascus and Aleppo, places he reputedly had visited before. On his return, Rumi also visited his Sheikh, Burhanaddin, in Kayseri, during which he completed a *chila* (a forty-day initiation) resulting in full-fledged acceptance into the Sufi path. Thus leaving him an everlasting impression, Sayyid Burhanaddin, who had introduced Rumi to the spiritual side of his father, passed away in Kayseri in 1240 or 1241 (638, according to the lunar calendar), and Rumi paid a visit to Sayyid Burhanaddin's grave.[5]

Mawlana Jalaladdin Muhammad Rumi, whose name was to become known throughout the world, had three sons and a daughter. The mother of Bahaaddin Muhammad (Sultan Walad) and his younger brother, Alaaddin Muhammad, was Gavhar Hatun, the daughter of Sharafaddin, of Samarqand, while the mother of his other son, Muzaffaruddin Amir Alim, and only daughter, Malika Hatun, was Kira Hatun, of Konya, whom Rumi married after the death of his first wife.

---

3   Aflaki, ibid., I, 1986:103,116.
4   ibid, 108,112.
5   ibid, 131.

During these years, Rumi, inspired with an erudite and Sufi character, spent prosperous times with students and friends alike, and established his prominence as one of the most important figures of Konya. The 29th of October, 1244 holds special importance in the life of Rumi, as it was on that day he met Shamsaddin Muhammad-i Tabrizi, or Shams of Tabriz, in Konya. The immediate effect of that meeting and the first words articulated by Shams is, on the account of Sultan Walad, as follows:[6]

> *Suddenly Shamsaddin came and reached him; shadow perished in the light of his light. The sound of love, free of tambourine and saz (a stringed musical instrument), came, emulating the world of love.*
>
> *He explained him in the states of the Beloved; thus ascended his secret to the highest of the highest, He said: You have become a hostage of the inward; but know that I am an inward.*

The acquaintance, which lasted close to two years, was not welcomed by the students and disciples of Rumi, who thought that they now no longer got from their master the attention they once had. Thus, owing to indignant complaints, Shams of Tabriz left Konya on the 10th or the 11th of March, 1246 (21 Shawwal 643), beginning a separation that put an end to a sixteen-month period which had begotten a remarkable devotion and love between the two; in short, it was a separation that would affect Rumi tremendously. As a result, the disciples who hoped to regain the Rumi "of old" by this forced departure became regretful of their actions.

## THE SUN SETS

Around 15 months later, in 1246 or 1247 (644, according to the lunar calendar), Shams returned from Damascus accompanied by Sultan Walad, who had been sent by Rumi for his deliverance. Before long, however, in 1247 or 1248 (645, according to the lunar calendar), Shams disappeared indefinitely. It has hesitantly been report-

---

6    Sultan Walad, *Ibtidaname*, quatrain 4335-4338, trns. Abdülbaki Gölpınarlı, Ankara, 1976:249.

ed that a group, which included the younger son of Rumi, Alaaddin, allegedly murdered Shams, although Sultan Walad, while speaking of his experiences of the event, does not mention it.[7] The years spent with Sheikh Salahaddin (d. 29 December 1258) and Husamaddin Chalabi, following two more visits to Damascus in the hope of locating Shams, proved prosperous for both Rumi and those around him. It should also be mentioned that during this period, Rumi wed his son with Fatima Hatun, the daughter of Sheikh Salahaddin.

Rumi, while 68 years of age according to the lunar calendar, and 66 according to the solar calendar, walked to his Beloved, on the 17th of December, 1273 (5 Jamaziyalahir 672). His successor, Husamaddin Chalabi, then passed away on the 3rd of October, 1284 (22 Shaban 683), approximately 11 years after Rumi's death.[8]

Rumi's loyal son, Sultan Walad, departed from physical existence on the 11th of October 1312. Sultan Walad and the remaining children of Rumi, scholar Alaaddin Chalabi (d. 1262), an official of the Seljuk Turks, Amir Alim Chalabi (d. 1277), and the wife of the Konyan trader, Shihabaddin, Malika Hatun (d. 1306), are all buried around Rumi under the Green Dome.

Throughout his life, Rumi enjoyed the enormous adulation and respect of the statesmen of the Seljuk Turks. For instance, Sultan Izzaddin II and Sultan Ruknaddin Kilich Arslan IV, who ruled independently and jointly between 1246 and 1264, used to frequently visit Rumi, attending his talks. Ruknaddin Kilich Arslan was, in fact, a disciple of Rumi, and among those Rumi addressed as "my son."[9] Muinaddin Parwana, who held power for 15 years, equally displayed immense respect for Rumi. The same holds true for two famous viziers, Majdaddin Atabek (d. 1277) and Sahib Ata Fakhraddin Ali (d. 1285).

Undeniably, throughout his life, Rumi met many scholars and gnostics. Sadraddin of Konya (d.1274), Qutbaddin of Shiraz (d.

---

7  See B.Furuzanfar, *Mawlana Jalaladdin*, trns. F.N.Uzluk, Istanbul, 1986:103-107.

8  Aflaki, II, 1987:144.

9  Aflaki, I, 1986:87; Turan, Osman, *Selçuklular Zamanında Türkiye* (Turkey during the Seljuk Turks), Istanbul, 1993:531-532.

1310), Fakhraddin-i Iraqi (d. 1283), Sheikh Najmaddin-i Razi (d. 1256), Qadi Sirajaddin of Urmiyah (d. 1283) and Safiyaddin of Hind (d. 1315) are included among those that spent time in Konya during the days of Rumi and actually met him.

Feeling a close proximity towards the Sufis before him, Rumi mentioned many of their names in his works. The examples of the love and ecstasy which encompassed Rumi's works were articulated by Ahmad-i Gazzali (d. 1123 or 1124) and the illustrious poets, Sena'i (d. 1131) and Sheikh Attar (d. 1220). Thus, the impressions of this tradition on the works of Rumi, and their mutual characteristics, should not be ignored.

Owing to his scholarly activities, Rumi is regarded among the noteworthy scholars of the Hanafi Jurisdiction.[10] Rumi, in possession of scholarly traits, is famous for saying, "Lest we become unworthy of the monthly salary of *fatwa* (verdicts according to Islamic jurisprudence), no matter which state I may be in, do not hinder anyone coming to ask for a *fatwa*." He is even reputed to have written verdicts during whirling and rapture.[11]

His depth of knowledge is evident in his extant Arabic and Persian poetry and prose, embellished by thousands of Qur'anic verses and hadiths (sayings of the Prophet Muhammad, peace be upon him). It is obvious that the love of poetry, predominant throughout society during his lifetime, was also deeply rooted in Rumi, as this explains his recitals of many Arabic and Persian *divan*s. Doubtless, he is the greatest representative of the road paved by Sufi poets Senai and Sheikh Attar, whom Rumi emulated in articulating his inherent feelings of love and ecstasy.

As a personality in whom gnosis poetic feelings amalgamated, Rumi dealt closely with everyday social problems, propounding convincing solutions to the predicaments of the human soul. The state

---

[10]  For instance al-Quraishi, Muhyiddin Abu Muhammad (1297-1374), *al-Jawahiru'l-Muziyya fi Tabaqati'l-Hanafiyya*, I-IV, pbl. Abdulfattah Muhammad al-Halawi, no.III, 1993:343-346.

[11]  Sipahsalar, 1977:98; Aflaki, I, 1986:306.

of love and rapture, which he carried incessantly, never isolated him from society or its problems. Thus, his legacy of works, comprising *Masnavi*, *Divan-i Kabir*, *Fihi Ma Fihi*, *Majalis-i Saba* and *Maktubat*, is filled with testimonies and examples.

According to what has been narrated, Mawlana Jalaladdin Muhammad Rumi, known also as Mevlevi, Hudavandigar, and Molla-i Rum, in addition to the epithets Balkhi, Rumi and Konavi, said:

> *In man, there are two great signs: one is knowledge, the other is altruism. Some have knowledge but no altruism. Some have altruism but no knowledge. Glory to the possessors of both.*[12]

Ülker Erke's miniature of the main Mevlevi Lodge where Rumi is buried

---

[12] Aflaki, I, 1986:331.

"... I am dust on the path of Muhammad, the Chosen One."

# INTERVIEW WITH MEVLEVI SHEIKH ŞEFİK CAN

by Nuriye Akman

T he last spiritual master of the Mevlevi sheikh tradition, Şefik Can, passed away at the age of 96, at his home in Suadiye, Istanbul, on January 23, 2005. *Zaman*'s Nuriye Akman had the last interview with him. Can, the late *Masnavi* reciter and spiritual head (*sar-tariq*) of the Mevlevis, shared with us some interesting insight in this interview, and also expressed his last will.

I got acquainted with Rumi and loved him thanks to the translations and interpretations of his works by Şefik Can. Whenever I take the *Masnavi* or other books, including some of its verses, in my hands, I send my sincerest gratitude to Şefik Can and have remained thankful to him over the years. I do not know why I have delayed my desire to interview him until last summer when I went to his house in Şaşkınbakkal on the spur of the moment as it was not on my agenda to do so. Yet our talk lasted for hours due to the depth of the issues, as well as the difficulties caused by his old age and physical discomforts.

Actually, if it hadn't been for Nur Artıran, his student and spiritual daughter, who was always by his side over the years, and to whom he entrusted his duties after his death, as outlined in his will, I honestly could not have held our interview so fluently and thus presented it to you. His ears heard so little that Ms. Artıran was pressed to repeat each one of my questions, one-by one, into her spiritual master's ears, a couple of times, as if she were spelling them. When replying, he spoke in a very low voice, and Ms. Artıran's task was to translate his answers in a way that I could understand. Later, after replaying the recording for myself, I received further help from Ms. Artıran in re-assembling the interview, because the deceased wanted to give such comprehensive answers to my questions that he often made deep dives into complementary topics which supported the main subject but sometimes made it difficult for me to follow his line of logic. Thus, before beginning this report, I would like to sincerely express my gratitude to Ms. Artıran, who was very well acquainted with the language of the deceased, both literal and spiritual. Perhaps learning that he has now given the moral entrustment he received from his master, Tahir'ul Mevlevi, to a female Mevlevi, might surprise some people. Yet, Can wanted to see Artıran become a *postnishin* of a women's sama group and hold talks about transmitting what is received from God to people, with love coming to bear at every stage.

Ultimately, I believe that my holding the last interview with Can was a rare gift allotted to me by God, so that sharing his will and point of view with the rest of the world, as related in this interview, has effectively become my responsibility. For Can was the last Mevlevi sheikh, a devout follower of Rumi and someone who not only knew the fundamentals of Mevlevi order best, but who also lived it best. I actually kept this interview for a whole summer because I was thinking that the most appropriate time to publish it would be just after the Shab-i Arus, the night Rumi returned to the Creator, celebrated on December 17th every year. However, as he was so ill during those days, I felt that it would be more appropriate to postpone it until now, wherein it has become today's grant.

――――――◆◆◆――――――

*Sir, how did you get acquainted with Rumi?*

I am the son of a town mufti. I was born in the town of Tebricik, in Erzurum [Turkey], and later my father became the mufti of the town. My father was interested in literature very much. He was both a valuable religious scholar who graduated from *madrasa* (university of theology) and an important mufti of that era. He was also an intellectual who taught at Dar'ul Muallim, the school for teacher training. My father taught me Arabic and Persian before I started school, but I can say that I really learned how to speak with the words of Rumi. Many of Rumi's poems that I know by heart are actually poems my father taught me in those days, and my closeness to Rumi began with my father's love for Rumi, which affected me deeply. Then, because of World War I, we left everything, moved to Sivas, and then to Yozgat. After having already been in too many places, we moved again because of the savagery of the war, and finally arrived at the town of Yıldızeli, somewhere between Sivas and Tokat, so I saw and experienced all the pains of war when I was just a child. My father was appointed the mufti of Yıldızeli right after we had just arrived. While I was attending primary school, my father made me memorize verses from Hafız, Sadi and Rumi, and I read *The Gulistan of Sadi*. When I graduated from primary school, my father taught me the masterpieces of these three wise and holy men.

Later on, I attended a military school in Tokat, and then the Kuleli Military High School, in Istanbul. I graduated from high school and the Military Academy, and became an army officer; however, there was a great desire in me to become a teacher. This was because the love for books, science, teaching and learning that I saw in my father, who was my first guide and spiritual master, had been passed on to me as well. I secretly attended literature courses in the Department of Turkish Literature at Istanbul University. When my secret was exposed, they took me from there and assigned me to a unit in a town called Vize, in Thrace, but I did not give up this love of mine even there. One day, I wrote a letter expressing my love for teaching to the commander of my unit and asked him to give me permission to complete my undergraduate education, and later, I passed the teachers' exam with the permission of my commander. Yet, to become a teacher, I had to complete a two-year internship. That's why they assigned me to Kuleli Military High School, so that I might complete my internship under the supervision of Tahir'ul Mevlevi, who was then teaching there.

That was how I first met master Tahir'ul Mevlevi during those times, and I had the honor of accompanying and serving him for 16 years. Look at the will of God, that I received both my material and spiritual diploma at the hands of Tahir'ul Mevlevi! This was indeed a great favor of God towards me. My first spiritual teacher was my late father; however, Tahir'ul Mevlevi was my second master, whom I loved as much as my father. He lighted my way to Rumi and guided me with his experience. Certainly, Tahir'ul Mevlevi's love for Rumi had a great influence on me. That's why I bought all the world classics, the works of the most famous poets, and I read them all. I dedicated my whole life to reading, and I eventually established a personal library of 10,000 books. Meanwhile, I set my heart on ancient Greek and classical Latin literature, and I even wrote a book on classical Greek mythology. I searched and read all the world literature, and I studied everything I read. My purpose in telling all this is simply to explain that I did not have merely a blindfolded spiritual attachment to Rumi.

*Sir, is the quatrain "Come, come whoever you are" understood correctly by contemporary people?*

This quatrain does not belong to Rumi, and this is already known by everyone. The library official at the *dargah*, the Mevlevi dervish

lodge, the late Necati Bey, had seen this quatrain written in old calligraphy on a sheet. Without searching for its origin, he spread the
rumor everywhere that it was a Rumi quatrain, whereas this quatrain
actually belongs to someone else in an anthology called *Harabat*,
compiled by Ziya Pasha. I saw that in another handwritten quatrain
as well; nevertheless, because Rumi has many quatrains like this one,
and even some more enthusiastic ones, it might also be accepted as
a Rumi quatrain. This is not very important, in fact. The main problem regards those who are unaware of the spirit of this quatrain and
take it on the surface, in addition to those who contributed to this
misunderstanding:

> *Come, come whoever you are*
> *Wanderer, worshipper, lover of living, it doesn't matter,*
> *Ours is not a caravan of despair*
> *Come, even if you have broken your vow a thousand times*
> *Come, yet again, come, come*

This specifically signifies the Qur'anic verse, *Say: "O My servants
who have transgressed against their souls! Do not despair of God's Mercy.
Surely God forgives all sins. He is indeed the All-Forgiving, the All-
Compassionate"* (Zumar 39:53), as well as all Qur'anic verses that
have God's address to, "O ye people." The point is that it does not
matter how sinful a person is, if one sincerely repents and asks God
for forgiveness, he or she will be cleansed of sins. Now Rumi means:
"O human, your heart is full of idols. Even if it is full of worldly idols
and every side of you is stigmatized with earthbound and corporeal filth, do not fall into despair. Come to our *dargah*, take the ax of
love and faith and break the idols inside you. If you drink alcohol,
come and discipline your ego at our *dargah*, hit that bottle on a
stone, and then drink the sacred wine. Come and cleanse yourself
with the water of the truth in our hands, get purified from your
filth and become clean."

He does not say "Come, our *dargah* is available for everything.
Do the things in our *dargah* that people outside do not accept, and
we will welcome it." Yet, people misinterpret it in this way so that

constantly reading this quatrain has had some negative effects on certain people. Through this wrong interpretation, they recognize Rumi in erroneous ways, perceiving him as a materialist who believes in the eternity of the world and rejects the other world, as well as being someone who believes that the soul dies together with the body. Alternately, they perceive him to be of another sect or another path, as if Rumi tolerates and accepts everything that God does not accept and that the Prophet does not find appropriate. Is such a thing possible? Rumi wrote: "I am the slave of the Qur'an for as long as I am living. I am dust on the path of Muhammad, the Chosen One." In one of his sayings, the Prophet Muhammad says that if people repent and ask God for forgiveness, but yet commit the same sin again, they would become more sinful. If you deny your oaths a hundred times and this is perceived as insignificant, then is this appropriate in Islamic belief? So those who are unaware of the spirit and essence of this verse, and who take it only as a face value, would definitely recognize Rumi wrongly. Yet didn't Rumi say anything else? Why doesn't someone read the quatrain in which he says, "I am the slave of the Qur'an for as long as I am living. I am dust on the path of Muhammad, the Chosen One"? Doesn't this describe Rumi? To understand the other quatrain, one has to think deeply. But because no one can bear that, it seems suitable to everyone's path.

*What kind of a person is Rumi in your eyes?*

Actually, we are not up to understanding and describing him thoroughly. That's why everyone comprehends and talks about Rumi according to their particular understanding and intuition, and they say what they see in their own mirrors. Great saints are like oceans and we are like little drops of water beside them. Just as a little drop cannot grasp a whole sea, it also cannot describe it correctly. Rumi, who himself saw and knew all these centuries ago, had described himself in one of his quatrains as follows: "I am the slave of the Qur'an for as long as I am living. I am dust on the path of Muhammad, the Chosen One. If anyone interprets my words in any other way, I deplore that person and I deplore his words." This quatrain is a very clear document about Rumi's path that would enable everyone to understand him. We commemorate him as the sultan of lovers. Because he says:

> *Our mother is love! Our father is love!*
> *We are born from love! We are love!*
> *All loves constitute a bridge leading to the Divine love.*
> *To love human beings means to love God.*

We cannot finish describing his humility and modesty for ages, and it is impossible to conclude it. We do not have any right to say anything to those who say they are on his path; however, look at the words of that great person, who is an example of humanity: "They value my turban, my robe and my head, all three of them, at one *dirham* (a small currency unit) or somewhat less. Haven't you ever heard my name in this world? I am nothing, nothing, nothing." Here is a clear sign of the modesty of Rumi, a great saint. Yet being nothing, realizing this nothingness, and continuing to walk on that path is not easy. Rumi himself says that he could not completely describe a human being, even if he tried until the Judgment Day. Then how could I ever describe Rumi, an exemplary human being? Yet again, a great saint describes this great saint best. Abdurrahman Jami once said: "*Masnavi* is enough to prove the value of that unique sultan of the world of meaning. What can I say about the quality and superiority of that great being? He is not a prophet, but has a book."

*We know that you ascended to the post a few times together with Selman Tüzün for the "Shab-i Arus" ceremony in Konya in the 1960s. Why did you withdraw from the post later on and not continue on this mission?*

I could not ascend to that post in Konya later on as a favor of God. If I had continued this mission, I would have continued to live as a ceremonial sheikh. Hence, I could not have had the chance to carry out studies on Rumi's masterpieces; since in my opinion, I have spent many of my years simply trying to prepare these works to serve

Rumi's followers. Books have always been the most important part of my whole life. For this reason, our Master Rumi gave me permission and allowed me to study his works, effectively preventing me from spending time for other things. In this way, he taught me to engage in a good service through his own works. And no matter how much I thank God for this bestowal, it will never be enough.

Appeared on *Zaman* Daily
January 31, 2005

# RUMI AND SUFISM

## Selahattin Hidayetoğlu

R umi's Sufi path is never an uninspired system of knowledge or an imaginary idealism; conversely, his understanding of Sufism is the act of maturing in the world of gnosis, realization, love and rapture.

Rumi perennially sees the realities of life, accepting them entirely without desisting from them. He objects to idleness and total detachment from life; and he revives a life within life itself, attested by his definition of the world, which divulges his Sufi path:

> *What is the world? It is being heedless of God. Fabric, money, conducting trade through measuring and weighing, and women; is not the world.*
> *The wealth you obtain to spend in the way of religion has been blessed by the Prophet as "Splendid Wealth!"*
> *Water inside the ship means destruction. Water beneath the ship, however, will assist it in its movement.*
> *Only by virtue of extirpating the love of riches from the heart did Solomon assume the tag "poor,"*
> *The pitcher, with a closed lid, sailed above the deep and boundless water, as it was filled with air.*
> *Indeed, so long as man carries the air of poverty, he will float above the sea of earth, eluding immersion.*
> *Even if the whole World is part of his property, this wealth, in his eyes, is a mere nothing.* [1]

## PURPOSE IN RUMI'S SUFI PATH

In Sufism, the purpose is servanthood and annihilating the self in the divine will:

---

[1] Rumi, *Masnavi*, Vol. I,

*It is, in fact, He, God, Who is the owner of riches and sovereignty; to whosoever pays homage to Him, He will indeed grant hundreds of riches and kingships, let alone this world created of dust.*

*But a prostration in His presence seems to you sweeter than two hundred states and kingdoms.*

*"I want neither wealth, nor property, nor a state and kingship. Just grant me that state of prostration, and that will do," you will beg, weeping and moaning.* [2]

*What you call a throne is none but a wooden trap. You regard your position as ultimate, though you are stranded outside the door...*
*Give that fallacious kingship to God, so He can bestow you with a true kingship everyone will acknowledge.* [3]

*Extinct, is the way to Divine Presence, unless through extinction.* [4]

*Those who roam at the door, accentuating "I" or "We," will be exiled, to roam forever at the station of La (negation word in Arabic for "no" or "non-existence").* [5]

*Whosoever liberates from the ego will obtain the entire egos; and as an opponent of himself, will become a friend of all.* [6]

*What an excellent ride the mule of extinction is. If you have become extinct, it will carry you to the station of being.* [7]

## LOVE IN RUMI'S SUFI PATH

Divine Love is the cause of creation, the doctor of all diseases, the cure of disdain and selfishness and the lotion of agony. How beautifully Rumi enunciates the Sufi concept that, "love is the very meaning of creation and life," through the subsequent words:

---

[2]  Rumi, ibid., Vol. IV, 664-666.
[3]  Rumi, ibid., Vol. IV, 661, 2778.
[4]  Rumi, ibid., Vol. VI, 232.
[5]  Rumi, ibid., Vol. I, 2665.
[6]  Rumi, ibid., Vol. IV.
[7]  Rumi, ibid., Vol. IV, 555.

*Love is that flame which, when it blazes up, burns everything except the Beloved.*[8]

*Love is among the attributes of God, Who is independent from need and want. Falling in love with others is thus a transitory fancy.*[9]

*O the medicine of our vanity and impunity, O our Plato! Our Galen! The body of dust has ascended to the heavens from love; the mountain has started to move, robust.*

*O Lover! Love has become the life of Mount Sina; the Sina, intoxicated while Moses has fainted senseless…*
*Whoever has no inclination to love is like a wingless bird; woe on to him.*[10]

As, in fact, the underlying principle is to reach to the Owner of the heart and become an essence, Rumi elegantly states:

*Let he who desires acquaintance with God sit in the presence of gnostics. Destroyed you are, indeed, if you split from this presence, as you are a particular, devoid of the universal.*[11]

*Distancing yourself from the presence of the gnostics, is in fact, distancing yourself from God.*[12]

*Persist around men of spirit, that you may obtain both grants and spoils, and become chivalrous.*
*A spiritless life in this body is, no doubt, like a wooden sword in a scabbard,*
*Valuable so long as it remains in the scabbard, only good for fire once removed,*
*Do not take the wooden sword to battle, examine it once, lest you may regret,*
*If it is wooden, then search for another, if diamond, then advance forward, blissfully.*

---

8   Rumi, ibid., Vol. V, 588.
9   Rumi, ibid., Vol. VI, 972.
10  Rumi, ibid., Vol. I, 23-26,31.
11  Rumi, ibid., Vol. II, 2163-2165.
12  Rumi, ibid., Vol. II, 2214.

*Diamond swords are in the arsenal of the gnostic; seeing them, for
you, is chemistry.
All those who know have expressed this as such and only as such: A
knower is a blessing for the Universes.*[13]

*Go not to the land of hopelessness, for there are hopes.
Refrain from darkness, for there are suns.
The heart will pull you toward the land of its companions; the flesh
will throw you into the dungeon of water and mud.
Be calm! Obtain your heart's sustenance from a person of heart;
feast your heart with it. Advance; learn triumph from its master.*[14]

## THE ADHERENCE OF RUMI TO ISLAMIC PRINCIPLES AND PROPHET MUHAMMAD (PBUH)

It is also important to attempt to articulate Rumi's understanding
of Islam. Incessantly conscious of the Qur'anic verse, *"The noblest
of you, in the sight of God, is the best in conduct,"*[15] Rumi was a person with abundant piety, who constantly abided by the etiquette set
forth by Qur'anic verdicts, abstained from things decreed forbidden by God, abandoned the pleasures of the flesh, and desisted from
the hindrances of attaining spiritual maturity; in sum, he endlessly
kept a distance from things that might have distanced him from
God.[16]

## RUMI NEVER DIGRESSED FROM THE ESSENTIALS OF ISLAM

Even during the tremendous rapture and ecstasy Rumi realized after
entrance into a realm through conversance with Shams—too far distant to be conceived or digested by his surroundings—he never took
even an infinitesimal step outside the essentials of Islam.[17]

---

13  Rumi, ibid., Vol. I, 711-717.
14  Rumi, ibid., Vol. I, 724-726.
15  Qur'an, 49:13.
16  Sipahsalar, Faridun b Ahmad, *Risala-i Sipahsalar ve Manaqim-i Hazrat-i Hudavandigar*, Dar Saadat, 1331:59-60.
17  Tarlan, Ali Nihat, *Mevlana* (Rumi), Hareket Yayınları, Istanbul, 1974:26.

## RUMI'S CONSCIENCE OF WORSHIP

Rumi says in the *Masnavi*, "Our Lord has decreed *'Prostrate, so you may draw near.'*[18] The prostration of our bodies is a cause for our spirits to draw near to God"[19]; thus, Rumi did not embrace divine love merely as an idea or concept. In actual fact, he exerted his obligations of worship with much zeal. The chronicler, Aflaqi narrates the following: "Upon hearing the *adhan* (the call to prayer), Rumi, pressing his hands against both his knees, would stand up, with all his formidability, and repeat three times: 'O with Whom our lives are verified! May Your name survive till eternity,'[20] followed by the concluding assertion, 'This prayer, fasting, pilgrimage and striving for God's cause are witnesses to faith. The presents, gifts and what is offered are witnesses to my love of You.'[21] 'Were Divine Love merely ideas or symbols, then the exterior form of Your prayer and fasting would no longer be; they would diminish.' Upon saying this, he would delve into prayer, full of humility and supplication."[22]

## RUMI, AN ADMIRER OF THE QUR'AN AND AN ADORER OF PROPHET MUHAMMAD (PBUH)

By the subsequent quartet, Rumi proclaims his unyielding adherence to the Qur'an and the Prophet Muhammad (peace be upon him):

> *So long as my life persists, I'm the servant of the Qur'an,*
> *A dust of the path of Muhammad, the Chosen,*
> *If one conveys contrary to my words,*
> *Disgusted I am from the conveyer and from the conveyed.*[23]

---

18  Qur'an, 96:19.
19  Rumi, *Masnavi* Vol. IV, 11.
20  Aflaki, Ahmad, *Ariflerin Menkıbeleri*, Milli Eğitim Basımevi, Istanbul, 1964, Vol. I, 3/1 06.
21  Rumi, *Masnavi* Vol. V, 183,185.
22  Rumi, ibid., Vol. I, 2625.
23  Rumi, *Divan-i Kabir, Rubaiyyat No:*133

## RUMI'S IDENTITY

Once the life and works of Rumi are thoroughly scrutinized, the following can be comfortably asserted. By eradicating his own knowledge in the knowledge of the Prophet Muhammad, his own gnosis in the gnosis of the Prophet Muhammad, and his personality in the personality of the Prophet Muhammad—in short, his entire existence in the existence of the Prophet Muhammad—Rumi ignited his spiritual identity with the dazzling flame of the Prophet's spiritual identity.[24] Rumi enunciated this reality through the following lines:

> *We, God's shadow, from the light of Mustafa,*
> *A priceless pearl dropped in ebony,*
> *How can everyone see us with a formal eye?*
> *We are the Majesty's light, appeared in water and mud.*[25]

## THE CENTER OF RUMI'S CIRCLE OF HUMAN PERCEPTION

It ought to be known that as a perfect guide, and within the framework of the purpose of creation, Rumi's duty was to strive to lead people to attain eternal bliss. Thus triggered by this holy endeavor, and aware of the commensurate responsibility, Rumi expressed the following: "We are like a compass; while one leg is firmly fixed on the Islamic Code of Law, the other sojourns the seventy-two nations."[26]

## THE SECRET, LIGHT, CONSCIENCE AND PEACE
## BEHIND HIS VAST TOLERANCE

Eternally, in the backdrop of Rumi's boundless tolerance, lays the secret of *Tawhid* (unity, God's Oneness), the illumination of the Qur'an, the conscience of faith, and the peace of Muhammadi ethics.

Evident is the fact that Rumi cleverly exhibited with his own lifestyle, the sublime tolerance imbibed from the joy of *Tawhid* and

---

[24] Beytur, Midhat Bahari, *Mesnevi Gözüyle Mevlana Şiirleri, Aşk ve Felsefesi*, Sulhi Garan Matbaası, Istanbul, 1965:133.
[25] Beytur, M. B., ibid., 1965:.99.
[26] Beytur, M. B., ibid., 1965:103.

the overflow of Muhammadi exuberance. What, in fact, constitutes the maturity and distinct quality in the personality of Rumi is his constant practice of what he preached, crystallizing his opinions with actions. It is useful to provide an example in relation to this point. Rumi was once performing *sama* (whirling) in congregation when suddenly, a drunken Christian joined him in the whirling and in the process, owing to his excitement, unremittingly bumped into Rumi, causing those present to begin vilifying the drunkard. Rumi, addressing the criticizers, asserted: "It is he who has drunk the wine, but it is you who are acting drunk." With the intention of exposing the drunkard, they responded: "He is a *tarsa* (Christian)," upon which Rumi, insinuating the other connotation of *tarsa* (fearful), stated: "If he is a *tarsa*, why aren't you?" Thus, those present eventually apologized for their misdeeds.[27]

---

27   Aflaki, Ahmad, *Ariflerin Menkıbeleri*, Milli Eğitim Basımevi, Istanbul, 1964, Vol. I, 3/291.

# SAMA AND THE SPIRITUAL SIGNS WITHIN

## Sezai Küçük

S*ama* or whirling, the name given to the *Sufi Mevlevi* ceremony popularized by Rumi and established by his name after his death, is literally an Arabic word, denoting a variety of meanings, such as listening, paying attention, lending an ear, the statement heard, good reputation, and remembrance. Terminologically, though, it has been the name given to listening to the musical melodies, and subsequently becoming enchanted, falling deep into ecstasy, moving arbitrarily to the sound, and to the standing *dhikr* (remembrance of God) performed by *sufis* amid a cyclone of rapture.[1] The *sama dhikr*, the ritual of whirling performed by Mevlevis on particular dates, is called *muqabala*, while the date itself is coined the "day of *muqabala*." *Sama*, as performed during the time of Rumi, out of an overflow of religious and spiritual feelings, and without being subject to any guidelines, eventually became institutionalized at the time of Sultan Walad and Ulu Arif Chalabi, continuing until the guidance of Pir Adil Chalabi, with performance becoming liable to teaching and learning. The various *Nat-i Sharif* (poetry in praise of Prophet Muhammad, peace be upon him) which was recited during the ceremonies of *Sama* up until the seventeenth century, made way for the later *Nat-i Sharif* composed by Itri, which subsequently became a permanent part of the ceremony.[2]

---

[1]  Uludağ, Süleyman, *Tasavvuf Terimleri Sözlüğü*, (Dictionary of Sufi Terms), Marifet Publishing, Istanbul 1991:422.

[2]  Gölpınarlı, Abdülbaki, *Mevlevi Adab ve Erkanı*, (Mevlevi Sufi Etiquettes and Principles), İnkılab ve Aka Publishing, İstanbul 1963:76-77; see also Gölpınarlı, A., *Mevlanadan Sonra Mevlevilik*, (Mevlevi Sufism after Rumi), İnkılab ve Aka Publishing, İstanbul, 1983:383.

The area where the *sama* is performed is called a *samahana*. In the Mevlevi Sufi Path, all things, whether these be the circular shape of the *samahana*, the costume of the dervishes, the color of the pelt used for seating or, for that matter, movements during the *sama*, collectively carry symbolic meanings.

*Sama*, performed in the time of Rumi upon the overflow of rapture, irrespective of a particular time,[3] began being performed after Rumi, usually following the Friday or noon prayer. Having performed the prayer on the day of *sama*, the *dervishes* then remain seated in full tranquility, waiting, as if it were their first entrance into the world of plurality, akin to the constituents of the universe itself.[4]

The *sama* ceremony commences with the *Nat-i Sharif*, in praise of the Prophet, composed in *rast* by Buhurizade Mustafa Itri, a renowned composer of the seventeenth century. *Nat-i Sharif* is a poem of Rumi's which glorifies Prophet Muhammad, peace be upon him, the noblest of creations and the cause of the existence of the universe. This *Nat* is recited by the *nathan* (one who recites the *nat*), standing and without music, while those present, in the hope of comprehending its profound meaning, give a full ear to the prose, and in doing so, providentially acquire a heart that remembers *(qalb-i hafiz)*, to attain the truth hidden in the core of matter that encompasses the visible universe.[5]

The *nat* is then followed by the sound of a *qudum*, an instrument similar to a tambourine, symbolizing God's command, "Be," which is the foundation of the creation of the universe, and which opens the curtain on the *nay taqsim*, an instrumental improvisation of the flute-like instrument, *nay*, which itself represents the Divine Breath, breathing the Spirit into the universe. The rhythm perme-

---

3    Gölpınarlı, A., *Mevlevi Adab ve Erkanı*, (Mevlevi Sufi Etiquettes and Principles), 1963:63-71

4    Al-Mevlevi, Haci Fayzullah an-Nakshibandi al-Muradi, *Tarcuma-i Risala-i Isharatu'l-Ma'nawiyya fi Ayini'l-Mevleviyye*, İstanbul, Matbaa-i Amira 1864:6; see also Gölpınarlı, *Mevlanadan Sonra Mevlevilik*, (Mevlevi Sufism after Rumi), 1983:371-372

5    Al-Mevlevi, ibid., 1864:7.

ating from the *nayzan* (nay players) during *taqsim* is, analogously, like a sign of the theophanies of God.[6]

Following this brief *nay taqsim*, and concomitantly with the first beat of the *qudum* by the *qudumzanbashi* (head *qudum* player), the Sheikh and the whirlers rise in unison, saying from their hearts, "Allah," and slapping the ground with their hands, a movement signifying initially God's creation of the lifeless body followed by its resuscitation from God's own breath, concluding with the constitution and the revivification of the universe. Because of its analogy to the resurrection of the lifeless body, it denotes both *hashr* and *nashr*[7]—resurrection and scattering in the Hereafter.

With the ensuing commencement of the *pashraw* (overture) following the *taqsim*, the Sheikh and the whirlers, corresponding with the tempo of the music, begin a circular walk, anti-clockwise, in the *samahana*. This circular walk, comprising three laps of the area, is called a *Dawr-i Walad*.[8]

The right half of the *muqabala* circle denotes the *Alam-i Mulk*, the Outward Universe, while the left half signifies the *Alam-i Malaqut*, the Inward Universe. The imaginary line separating these two halves, adjacent to the Sheikh's pelt and the door of the *samahana*, is called *hatt-i istiva*. While passing by this line, the *samazan*s (whirlers) offer an invocation, crossing over without stepping onto it. The first part of the *Mevlevi Sama*, called the *Dawr-i Walad*, was arranged in three laps by Rumi's son, Sultan Walad.[9]

The *Dawr-i Walad* comes to an end with the Sheikh taking his place at the pelt at the end of the third lap. Simultaneously, this walk symbolizes knowing the Ultimate Truth with *Ilma'l Yaqin* (cer-

---

6   Al-Mevlevi, ibid., 1864:7-8; see also Çelebi, Celalettin, B., "Sema" (Whirling), 2nd Rumi Congress Papers, Konya, 1986:204.

7   Al-Mevlevi, ibid., 1864:9

8   Uludağ, Süleyman, *Tasavvuf Terimleri Sözlüğü*, (Dictionary of Sufi Terms), Marifet Publishing, Istanbul 1991:85-86.

9   Al-Mevlevi, ibid., 1864:13.

tainty of knowledge), seeing with *Ayna'l Yaqin* (certainty of sight), and the ultimate realization through *Haqqa'l Yaqin* (certainty of truth).

Then the *nayzanbashi* (head nay blower) plays a short *taqsim* upon which the *samazan*s remove their black vests, which represent their outward existence. Again, symbolically, the birth into the truth is represented by the *samazan*, with a cross-arm stance—a posture denoting to the number "One," effectively alluding to the Oneness of God. Then, after having seen the Sheikh and kissed his hand one-by-one, in order, the *samazan*s receive the go-ahead to commence "whirling."[10]

The *sikka*, a headwear peculiar to the *samazan*s, symbolizes the vice of man or the tombstone of his "self," while the *tannura* represents the shroud of the "self," and the vest worn stands for the "self." While whirling, open-armed from right to left, the *samazans'* right hand faces the heavens, whereas the left is turned towards the ground, meaning, "We take from the Truth and disburse it to the public, desisting from usurpation for ourselves." The *samazan*s rotate around the area, akin to how the planets rotate around themselves and around the Sun. The idea of the *sama* is itself an expression of the composition of the universe, and within it man's resurrection, his movement triggered by the love of God, and his inclination towards the Universal Man, or *Insan-i Kamil*, by virtue of realizing his servanthood.[11]

The *sama* is comprised of four parts, each called the *salaam*. The *samazanbashi* maintains order by observing the circulation of the whirlers. The first *salaam* is the realization by man of his servanthood. The second, on the other hand, is the awe in front of the greatness and might of God. Successively, the third *salaam* is where this awe transforms to love, a prelude for the fourth *salaam*, which is the comprehensive understanding of the purpose of creation.

10  Gölpınarlı, Abdülbaki, *Mevlevi Adab ve Erkanı*, (Mevlevi Sufi Etiquettes and Principles), 1963:87

11  Çelebi, Celalettin B., "Sema" (Whirling), 2nd Rumi Congress Papers, Konya, 1986: 204.

Just as the fourth *salaam* begins, the *postnishin* (sheikh) makes a *charq* by way of moving slowly towards the middle of the *sama-hana* on the *hatt-i istiva*, without taking off his vest nor opening his arms. The sheikh's return to the pelt marks the end of this *taqsim*, which is subsequently followed by an *Ashr-i Sharif*, recital of some Qur'an. The *sama* ceremony then concludes with final prayers, the *Hu* (chanting of God's name), and closing salutations.[12]

By virtue of this ceremony, the phases of "*coming from Him and returning to Him,*" in addition to the levels of spiritual maturity, are elegantly exhibited.

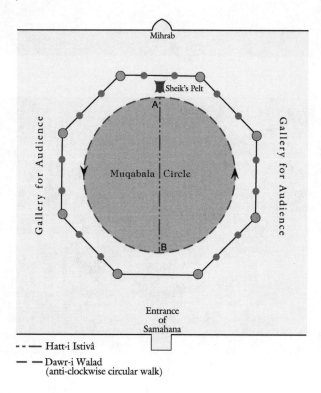

---

12  Gölpınarlı, A., *Mevlevi Adab ve Erkanı*, (Mevlevi Sufi Etiquettes and Principles), 1963:87-94; see also Çelebi, Celalettin B., Sema, "Sema" (Whirling), 2nd Rumi Congress Papers, Konya, 1986:205-206

Gallipoli Samahana, Turkey

# HISTORY OF MEVLEVI SUFISM

Nuri Şimşekler

C enturies ago, the arrow was pointing at a date, that of the 17th of December, 1273, just as the sun was setting on the West, radiating the horizon with its pulsating crimson, in preparation to rise, yet again, upon other provinces. Despite its seeming disappearance, the sun was merely completing its routine journey, on its destined path to illuminate the globe. Around about the same time, another sun, that of Rumi, ordained to enlighten the Earth by the grace of God and the activation of Shams, was proceeding forth, a departure which, while heralding a reunion with the Beloved, also carried glad tidings of an eternal rebirth soon to be revealed. Rumi, through the wonderful poetry he had uttered during his physical stay on Earth, emphatically accentuated that death is nothing but a fresh start, a mere return to the place of departure—or simply put, "Death is life; death is, indeed, life."

Rumi, having surpassed the levels of "knowledge" and "love" during the phases perhaps better known as pre-Shams and post-Shams, left a marvelous legacy of prose and poetry divulging mystical secrets during ecstatic moments of Divine enchantment, first and foremost headed by the masterpiece *Masnavi*, an astonishing hand guide to being human. Apart from these treasures, and perhaps more importantly, he bequeathed an Islam-centered way of life, whose core philosophy is to be, to quote the words of Rumi himself, "a servant of the Qur'an and a dust of the Prophet's path," a paradigm to be emulated by all Muslims.

Were these teachings, then, articulated furtively at times and explicitly at others, through clever allegory easily comprehendible by even the most oblivious, destined to complete their mission with

Rumi breathing his last? Or was this frame of mind, embedded in love and tolerance, doomed to fall into disrepute after being imparted through only a couple of generations? Rumi, in fact, hinted somewhat at the foregoing concern during his corporeal life, stating that, "the *Masnavi*, after us, will act as a guide and exhibit the true path to the perplexed," donating an enormous inheritance that, rather than falling into oblivion, has only grown in importance, and moreover, been recognized as a wonderful interpretation of the Qur'an.

## How did Mevlevi Sufism start?

For the purposes of guarding, continuing and serving the future generations, the philosophy of "the humane life" promulgated by Rumi, the *Mevlevi* tenets, were institutionalized by Rumi's son, Sultan Walad and the copier of the *Masnavi,* Husamaddin Chalabi, along with other disciples of the path, established a distinctive Sufi way. And while the rest of the devotees desirously anticipated that Walad would take the helm following Rumi's death, Walad never saw himself fit, nominating Husamaddin instead for the responsibility of guidance, thus gaining supremacy over his own self, and triumphing in a battle ardently emphasized by his father.

During the 11 years of his guidance, Husamaddin had the current Green Dome built, under which resides the tomb of Rumi, and gathered around him friends and disciples, profusely soothing eager hearts by virtue of Qur'an recitals and readings from the *Masnavi*, in congregations of pure gnosis, a method which was to become an imperative of the Mevlevi Sufism.

Following the passing away of Husamaddin, in 1284, Sultan Walad, 58 years of age at the time, assumed leadership, commencing a prosperous period of 28 years which was to become witness to a rapid growth in the number of affiliates, the strengthening of relations with the Seljuk court, and most importantly, the incorporation into the Mevlevi Sufism of *sama* (whirling), music and *Masnavihanlik* (the rendition of *Masnavi*), after regulating each practice in concordance with the principles of the Mevlevi path. The *adab* (manners) and *arkan* (principals) of Mevlevi Sufism, built in subsequent years upon these foundations, were to survive to our day with minimum alteration.

While the Mevlevi Way, under the helm of Sultan Walad, became subject to basic, central principles on the one hand, it spread in Anatolia on the other, primarily in chief cities such as Kirsehir, Amasya and Erzincan, by virtue of officially ordained assistants sent by the Sheikh himself. The very fact that these assistants were welcomed with utmost sympathy paved the way for the conquering of hearts through the wisdom of Rumi, *sama* and Sufi music in newly established Mevlevi centers—or, to use the original term, *zawiyas*.

By the time Sultan Walad walked to God in 1312, the foundations of the Way had been, for the most part, firmly established; thus, within this framework, the eternal beauty of Islam had begun to be presented to the multitudes of hopefuls in a way previously unknown. Long before succeeding his father, Sultan Walad, Ulu Arif Chalabi (d.1320) had already taken great leaps towards mastery, exerting diligent effort in spreading the tenets by journeying through Anatolia and Persia. The *Mevlevi Zawiyas* initiated in Karaman, Beyşehir, Aksaray, Aksehir, Afyon, Amasya, Nigde, Sivas, Tokat, Birgi, Denizli, Alanya, Bayburt, Erzurum and sequentially, Tabriz, were the legacy of these prosperous visits.

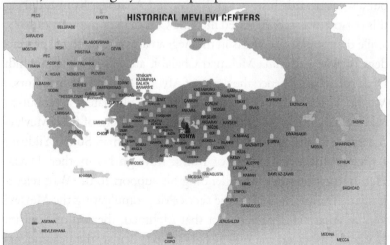

HISTORICAL MEVLEVI CENTERS

Despite their fervent desire to spread the teachings in concordance with the traditional heritage, Shamsaddin Abid (d. 1338)
and Husamaddin Wacid (d. 1342), after succeeding their brother,
Ulu Arif Chalabi, could only manage to guard and uphold this way
of love, owing to the rise in political strife in Anatolia at the time.
Their successors, Amir Adil Chalabi (d. 1368), Amir Alim Chalabi
II (d. 1395), and Arif Chalabi (d. 1421) faced similar political encum-
brances, and thus failed to extend the parameter of the way.

## THE RECONSTRUCTION OF THE MEVLEVI WAY

By the time Pir Adil Chalabi, the son of Amir Alim, assumed leadership of the Mevlevis in 1421, other institutionalized Sufi Paths,
primarily the Baktashiyya, Halwatiyya and Qadiriyya, had become
widespread. Thus, to distinguish the principles of the Mevlevi Way
from the rest, Pir Adil Chalabi decided to restructure the Way, including a rearrangement, in conformity with its original style, of the *sama*
(whirling), which had practically been left untouched since the
time of Sultan Walad.

The years spanning from the death of Pir Adil Chalabi, 1460
to 1509, marked the period of his son, Jamaladdin Chalabi, a half-
century that proved its significance not only for the Mevlevi Way,
but also as regards histories of Konya and Anatolia. Konya, during
this period, was incorporated into the Ottoman dominions (1467),
while the exceptional efforts in the Aegean area of a maternal descendent of Rumi, Dîvâna Mehmed Chalabi, and his disciple, Shahidi
Dede (d. 1550), opened the doors of Afyon, Denizli, Kütahya, Bursa,
Muğla, Isparta, Burdur, Aydın, Izmir–and ultimately, Istanbul–to
Mevlevi teachings, culminating in an establishment of fresh Mevlevi
centers within these localities. Again, the Ottoman Sultan Yildirim
Bayazid, also a descendent of Rumi, through his mother, Davlat
Hatun, took minute care in lending his support to the Way, relent-
lessly delivering himself to the service of promulgating the Mevlevi
Way in Anatolia. The very fact that Mehmed, the son of Yildirim
Bayazid, embraced the title "Chalabi," peculiar to the descendents

of Rumi, instead of the usual title, Sultan, certainly demonstrates his profound love and respect for the Mevlevi Way.

The sixteenth century, which witnessed the zenith of the Ottoman State, also saw full-fledged financial and political support of the Way by Sultan Selim I (r. 1512-1520), Suleyman the Magnificent (r. 1520-1566), and Selim II (r. 1566-1574), which the then-incumbent leaders, Husrav Chalabi (d. 1561) and Farruh Chalabi (d. 1591), utilized wholeheartedly to expand and strengthen the Mevlevi Way.

The onset of the seventeenth century saw the reign of a Mevlevi, Sultan Ahmad (r. 1603-1617), who, as one would expect, provided overwhelming support to the then-Mevlevi leader, Bostan Chalabi I, who, in turn, owing to popular encouragement of the Sultan and many statesmen, further revivified the Way during his 39 years at the helm, to such an extent that, by the time he breathed his last, the Mevlevi Way had become well-rooted in the Balkans, Egypt and Syria.

Bostan's successor, Abu Bakir Chalabi, was not as fortunate, however, and faced dire times during the reign of Sultan Murad IV (r. 1623-1640), who inveterately opposed not only the Mevlevis but also all Sufi movements in general. Even so, Sultan Murad, keen on destroying the Mevlevi center in Konya en route to Baghdad, recoiled from realizing his goal after undergoing a rather mystical experience at the center, after which he acquiesced in the Way and overwhelmed Abu Bakir Chalabi with presents, thereby bolstering the center with ceaseless funding.

After Abu Bakir Chalabi, Arif Chalabi (d. 1642) assumed leadership, succeeded by Hussein Chalabi, who served a further 24 years as leader of the Mevlevis. Marked by the reigns of Sultan Ibrahim (r. 1640-1648) and Mehmed IV (r. 1648-1687), and perhaps in line with the overall decline of the Empire, the Mevlevi Sufism failed to take fresh steps, and it was even prosecuted, at times, with allegations of political aspirations, especially during the leaderships of Hussein Chalabi (d. 1666) and later, Abdulhalim Chalabi (1679).

After Abdulhalim Chalabi's walk to eternity in 1679, his son, Kara Bostan Chalabi, succeeded him and strove to eradicate such unfortunate complications during his leadership. Kara Bostan Chalabi initially exerted a colossal struggle in hope of elevating the Mevlevi Way and succeeded in returning the Way to its glory days—a task in which he enjoyed great success. The Mevlevis had now begun to reassemble, not only in Konya but also in the other Mevlevi centers which, by now, were abundantly posited in the four corners of the Ottoman Empire. Long before Walad Chalabi's active participation in the Channel Operation, in Syria, during World War I, with the Mevlevi combatants, Kara Bostan Chalabi was even able to swiftly form a contingent to assist Suleyman II (r. 1687-1691) in his military expedition into the Balkans, eventually joining him near Edirne, in Balkan territory.

Reflecting on more recent times, we see another group of the Mevlevi combatants that included many prominent Mevlevi sheikhs who joined the Ottoman troops during World War I. They returned from Damascus without finding an opportunity to take part in active combat. During this time, Walad Chalabi, a poet by nature, was removed from his post, to be replaced by the former leader, Abdulhalim Chalabi, who concurrently during this period was also a

Mevlevi Troops during World War I

member of parliament representing Konya at the *Ottoman Majlis-i Mabusan* (General Assembly). Abdulhalim, having been able to serve a further year during this second term, was in due course replaced by Amil Chalabi. Elderly and burdened with grave health problems, Amil died within the year, after which Abdulhalim Chalabi, for the third and last time, was given the responsibility of leadership.

Prominent among the last *chalabi*s, and endowed with an animated personality, Abdulhalim served between 1920-25 in his third term, a period during which he entered his first position in the Turkish parliament as MP for Konya, then secured the election for the second President of the Assembly, after M. Kemal Ataturk. Chalabi had previously been awarded the Istiklal Medal by the Assembly, in honor of his invaluable services during the War of Independence. After Abdulhalim walked to eternity on the 12th of October, 1925, Walad Chalabi (Izbudak) assumed leadership for the second time.

The second term of Walad Chalabi, the MP for Yozgat and Kastamonu, who additionally translated the entire *Masnavi* from Persian into Turkish, could not last long either, as the *Mawlana Dargah* (center) suffered a similar fate as other such institutions around the country, in the face of the amendment pronouncing the closure of all *Takkas* and *Dargahs*, centers of Sufi ways. Out of his overflowing love for Rumi and the traditionally loyal Mevlevis, however, Ataturk, the founder of the Republic ordered a renovation of the *Dargah* in Konya to serve as a Museum, a command brought to fruition in 1927. Furthermore, before the death of Abdulhalim Chalabi (1925), Ataturk designated Abdulhalim's son, Mehmed Bakir Chalabi, as Sheikh of the *Mawlavihana* in Aleppo, the Mevlevi Way's official center until its abolishment by the Syrian Government in 1944.

During his stay in Aleppo, while assisting the Way in concordance with Mevlevi tenets, Mehmed Chalabi also attracted the exasperation of the French officials in Syria, owing to his vociferous participation in the bid to return the city of Hatay to Turkey. Chalabi, branded as a spy by both the French and the Syrians, was indefinitely prevented from reentering Syria after a family visit to Istanbul in

1937. Although his brother, Shamsul Wahid Chalabi, acted as his proxy in Aleppo, he was officially recognized as Sheikh only until the death of Mehmed Chalabi, in Istanbul, in 1943, after which the Syrian government closed the curtain on the *Mawlavihana* of Aleppo, in tandem terminating the official status of the Mevlevi sheikh there.

## A CONTEMPORARY PERSPECTIVE

After having rejected the Syrian Government's offer of returning the rich *waqf*s (foundations) of the *Mawlavihana* of Aleppo, on condition that they become subject to the Syrian Government, Jalaladdin Bakir Chalabi, son of Mehmed Chalabi returned to his motherland, settling in Istanbul, where until his death in 1996, he promulgated the ideas of Rumi domestically and internationally, in addition to conducting his other duties as ambassador of Turkish culture and tradition. The meticulous efforts of Jalaladdin Chalabi did not go unnoticed; he was, in fact, awarded the honorary doctorate title by Selçuk University in 1989.

After the death and subsequent burial of Jalaladdin Chalabi, Rumi's grandchild from the 21st lineage, in Üçler Cemetery, Konya, chiefly his son, Faruk Hemdem, his daughter, Esin Bayru, and the remainder of his children assumed the obligation of the Path. Making full use of contemporary technology, the Chalabi Family is now conveying the Way, and by the benefit of the Internet serving not only those in Turkey but also the entire globe in promulgating the wisdom of Rumi.

## THE MEVLEVI WAY AND ITS PURPOSE

The Mevlevi Way, from its establishment in the 1300s to its closure by the expedient of the amendment of 1925, has guided people to love and truth, not only in Anatolia but also in over 130 centers disseminated from Baghdad to Belgrade, to Mecca and Thessalonica, opportunely carrying into these lands Muslim cultural heritage through the priceless service it has rendered to fine arts. The crux of the Mevlevi Way is nothing other than the art of guiding people to initially discover their inner depths by way of self-training, rearing them to be harmonious with themselves and their ambiance, inculcating timely and precise tolerance, and teaching to judge not according to forms but meanings. Furthermore, it is a way that seeks to abandon idleness with the passionate desire to perpetually discover things anew, becoming beneficial to humankind through the constant rejuvenation of the self. What needs to be remembered, first and foremost, however, is that Mevlevi Sufism is Islam-centered.

Thus, the aim of the Mevlevi Way is to assist humankind—created by God in the form of "human," and concomitantly rendered the most noble of creatures—to live a humane life, which, as the term suggests, is distinct from that of animals or, for that matter, the "rebellious" Satan. Simpler put, human must desist from leading an animalistic life aimed toward appeasing sensuality and lust, and even more so, to avoid a diabolic life stemming from striving for the misery of the rest. The crucial aspect at this point is to delve into the core of Islam, taken in its extensive centrality by Mevlevi Sufism rather than a strictly traditional or formal acceptance. In the words of Rumi, this means not limiting the remembrance of God to only "five times a day," but instead being with Him constantly, including Him in the heart as an impetus behind absolutely every affair. Once one achieves this unity, one will perennially feel the Divine Presence, and thus feel delighted upon good acts but instantly repentant of those that are bad.

By the expedient of insidious examples, Islam, in recent years, has been the target of detrimental attempts to become portrayed globally as a religion of violence and terror. Mevlevi Sufism, among the groups to have understood and realized the true meaning of Islam, has attracted the close attention of non-Muslims owing to its historical reputation of desisting from conflict, to the effect that many non-Muslims have embraced Islam after having become conversant with Rumi and his philosophical legacy, Mevlevi Sufism. A wonderful example is the case of the French Professor, Eva de Vitray Meyerovitch (d. 1999), for whom the Way opened the door to Islam.

The conclusion reached by the British orientalist and Rumi researcher, Dr. Arthur J. Arberry, after years of research on Rumi's works, accentuates the importance of the ideas of Rumi insofar as humankind is concerned: "Rumi, 700 years ago, saved the world from immense turmoil. The only thing, in our day, that can save Europe is his works."

As evident from the foregoing examples and inferences, open for augment if one may wish, Rumi and his ideas occupy special importance among the best examples the Muslim world can present to the West, possessing a worth equally determined by aesthetics, method, and the true comprehension and conveyance of Islam, which indeed are aspects that are, by the same token, applicable to Turkey, since in Mevlevi Sufism, there is no compulsion, there is only, as existent in the core of Islam, being an example, and consequently exhibiting the beautiful aspects of religion, as well as its deepest principles.

# THE MAWLANA MUSEUM

Erdoğan Erol

While the current location of the Mawlana *Dargah* (Rumi Convent), now serving as a museum, was the rose garden of the Seljuk Palace in Konya, it was presented as a gift to Rumi's father, the *Sultanu'l-Ulama* (the Sultan of Scholars), Bahaaddin Walad, by the Seljuk Sultan, Alaaddin Kay Qobad.

Upon his death on the 12th of January, 1231, the Sultanu'l-Ulama was buried in his current resting place in the tomb, which was, in fact, the first burial in the rose garden.

Following the death of *Sultanu'l-Ulama*, and despite the insistent requests of his companions, who desired to build a tomb to him, Rumi declined the offer, saying, "Could there be a better tomb than the dome of sky?" Rumi's son Sultan Walad, however, accepted the offer of those wishing to erect a tomb over his own father's grave, following his death on the 17th of December, 1273. Thus, an

Green Dome and
the interior of the Museum

architect, Badraddin, of Tabriz, at a cost of 130,000 Seljuk dirhams, eventually constructed the tomb known as *Kubba-i Hadra* (the Green Dome), on four massive pillars. Building activities continued, with gradual additions until the nineteenth century. And the financial construction which began with the erection of the tomb of Rumi in 1273 concluded with the erection of the Dervish Rooms in 1854.

The Mevlevi Convent and Tomb began its service as a museum under the name *"Konya Asar-i Atika Müzesi,"* that is, "The Konya Museum of Ancient Relics," in 1926, which was eventually changed to the "Mawlana Museum," following the re-evaluation of the museum's public display in 1954.

Although the museum's area, including its garden, was formerly 6,500 square meters, it has now reached 18,000 square meters, with newly expropriated surroundings redesigned as a rose garden.

The entrance to the courtyard of the museum is through the *Dervishan Door*. Positioned along the east-west axis of the courtyard are the rooms of the dervishes. After the southern *Matbah* (kitchen) and *Hurram Pasha Tomb*, the courtyard ends with the *Hamushan Door* leading to the *Üçler Cemetery*. Lying east of the courtyard, on the other hand, is the main building, which includes the tomb of Sinan Pasha, Fatma Hatun and Hasan Pasha, as well as the *Samahana*, *Masjid* and *Mawlana Tomb*, including the graves of members of his family.

The roofed *Shadirwan* (fountain), the Pool of *Shab-i Arus* (wedding night), built by the Ottoman Sultan Selim I in 1512, and the spring named *Salsabil* (the softly flowing fountain), found at the northern end of the courtyard, add extraordinary color to the ambiance.

## THE *TILAVAT* ROOM

*Tilavat*, an Arabic word, denotes the recital of the Qur'an using a beautiful voice and observing its guidelines. The name of the room comes from its past use for the recital of the Qur'an. Currently, it is employed for calligraphy, precisely under the name of *"Hat Dairesi"* (Calligraphy Room).

The Calligraphy Room contains the works of renowned calligraphers, like Mahmud Jalaladdin, Mustafa Rakim, Hulusi and Yesarizade, in addition to a gold-embossed tablet written by the Ottoman Sultan Mahmud II.

The following couplet in Persian, belonging to Molla Jami, can be cited on a panel written by the pen of Yesarizade Mustafa Izzed Efendi:

> *Ka'batu'l-ushâq bâshad in maqâm*
> *Har ki naqis amad injâ shud tamâm*
>
> *This station has become the Ka'ba of lovers*
> *Whoever comes here deficient will become complete.*

## HUZUR-I PIR (TOMB)

The entrance into the hall of the tomb is through the silver door built by Hasan Pasha, son of Sokullu Mehmed Pasha, in 1599. The two display windows found inside exhibit the oldest manuscripts of Rumi's most renowned works, *Masnavi* and *Divan-i Kabir*. The hall of the tomb is covered by three small domes, of which the third, called the Post Dome, is northerly adjacent to the Green Dome.

The tomb of Rumi's father,
Bahaaddin Muhammad (left),
Calligraphy from The Tilavat
Room (above)

An elevated barrier on the east, south and north surrounds the Hall. The two barriers, found in two pieces on the north, contain the sarcophaguses of six Sufis of Khorasan.

Two panels, again found in this area, are pivotal in terms of elucidating Rumi's philosophy and system of thought:

The first panel is in Turkish:

*"Ya olduğun gibi görün. Ya göründüğün gibi ol"*
*"Appear as you are, or be as you appear."*

The second is a Persian quartet of Rumi, about acceptance and forgiveness, which can be translated into English as such:

*Come, come whoever you are*
*Wanderer, worshipper, lover of living, it doesn't matter,*
*Ours is not a caravan of despair*
*Come, even if you have broken your vow a thousand times*
*Come, yet again, come, come*

Found on the elevated barrier, surrounding the hall on the east and south, are sixty-five graves, of which fifty-five are of the descendents of Rumi and his father Bahaaddin Walad, including 10 females, in addition to another 10 belonging to renowned Mevlevis, such as Husamaddin Chalabi, Salahaddin Zarqubi, and Sheikh Karimuddin. The visitor will note that the *Sikka* (Mevlevi headdress) has not been placed on the sarcophagi belonging to the females.

Right beneath the Green Dome are the graves of Rumi and his son, Sultan Walad. The marble sarcophagi found on the graves were built by Sultan Suleyman the Magnificent in 1565. The *Pushida* (quilts) embroidered with golden lace were placed on the sarcophagi during the reign of Sultan Abdulhamid II, in 1894.

The sarcophagus found above that of Bahaaddin Walad, whose peculiar upright position led to claims like, "The father has risen upon his son's entrance," is actually a Seljuk masterpiece built for Rumi in 1274. After Sultan Sulayman placed a new marble sarcophagus on the graves of Rumi and his son Sultan Walad, the wooden sarcophagus was removed and placed on the grave of Rumi's father, who, until then, did not have a sarcophagus.

## SAMAHANA

The *Samahana* Section, along with the *Masjid*, was built by Sultan Suleyman in the sixteenth century, in which "*sama*" (whirling) continued until the *Dargah* was turned into a museum in 1926. The Pulpit for the Recital of Naat (poems) in praise of the Prophet Muhammad, the *Mutrib* Room, where the musicians sit, and the *Mahfils* (circles of men and women) have all been authentically preserved, with historical rugs, Mevlevi musical instruments, and metal and wooden handcrafts exhibited in displays and on appropriate walls of the *Samahana*.

## *MASJID* (MOSQUE)

In addition to the *Charagh Door*, the *Huzur-i Pir* section, where the graves are located, may also be employed as an entrance to the *Masjid*. The *Muezzin*'s (caller's) Pulpit, and likewise the pulpit of the *Masnavihan* (Masnavi Reciter), have both been preserved in their original states.

While there is a display of exquisite rugs and wooden doors by the southern wall of the *Masjid*, by the same token, there are inestimable examples of leather bindings, calligraphy, and gilding in displays dispersed in the various corners of the *Masjid*.

## THE *KUMASH* (FABRIC) SECTION AND DERVISH CHAMBERS

Surrounding the east and north directions of the front courtyard of the convent are seventeen rooms or chambers, each with a small dome and chimney, built by Sultan Murad III, in 1584, for the purpose of accommodating dervishes.

The four chambers positioned on the right of the entrance are currently utilized for administrative purposes. The first two of the

remaining thirteen chambers on the left of the entrance are exhibited with their original apparatus, as chambers of the *Postnishin*
(Sheikh), and also the *Masnavihan*.

The two chambers located at the very end are reserved for the
books donated by the late Abdulbaki Gölpınarlı and Dr. Mehmet
Önder, from their invaluable collections. The chambers currently
serve as libraries.

By removing the separating walls between the remaining nine
rooms, two long corridors attached to one another result, which are
generally utilized for the presentation of slide shows. The display
windows, posited in the window openings and thresholds facing the
corridor, exhibit precious historical artifacts transferred from the convent to the museum belonging to the Mevlevi ethnography, such as
the *Pazarci mashasi* (tongs), *muttaqa* (a tool used in retreat) and *nafir*
(an instrument of Sufi music), in addition to the exceptionally valuable garments of Bursa found in the museum's collection.

## THE MATBAH (KITCHEN)

The *Matbah*, built by Sultan Murad III, and found in the south-
west corner of the museum, operated as the kitchen of the convent
until its transformation into a museum in 1926.

Subsequent to its renovation in 1990, the section was redecorat-
ed with mannequins and employed to exhibit the traditional and
authentic style of cooking and *somat* (etiquette of eating) from the
floor-table. The *nav-niyaz*, another function of the *matbah*, is further
illustrated through the mannequins, as the Mevlevi candidate is seated
on the *Saka* (pelt), while by the Whirling Nail used for whirling practice, the Elder is instructing the art of whirling to a dervish hopeful.

# PART III

Rumi in the West

# MAWLANA
# FROM A EUROPEAN POINT OF VIEW

Peter H. Cunz

To write about Rumi and his contributions today is sending a drop of water into the ocean. Publications of selected verses, poems, or commentaries about Rumi's literary works have increased exponentially over the last ten years. Particularly in North America and Europe there have been many books and articles, of a variety of quality, that have been published. This is a sign of the hidden longing of a spiritually disorientated culture.

In Europe, the name "Rumi" is more widespread than the honorary title "Mawlana." Only those Europeans who have some background knowledge about the works of Mawlana will know him by this title. There are so many different people in Europe who are interested in Mawlana: experts of the Middle East, philosophers, humanists, psychologists, artists, theologians, and those who are searching for a spiritual way—they all find inspirations and stimuli in Mawlana's works. In Europe, the universal dimension of Mawlana's message is always emphasized, and his path of love within Sufism has attracted millions of people from all over Europe.

The Europeans' request to comprehend the message of Mawlana, whose soul and thinking was molded by Islam, without a corset of some dogmatic interpretations, is a legitimate demand. Europe is a product of the Enlightenment of the seventeenth and eighteenth centuries; this revived the appreciation of democracy and prepared the ground for secularization. The Europeans are fundamentally convinced of the autonomy of human reason: "Reason is the only and last authority that determines methods, truth, and error of every single idea and also the norms of ethical, political, and social action" (*Meyer's Encyclopedia*). But, nevertheless, the Europeans also experience a yearning for God and some of them try to quench the thirst in their hearts by translating the works of great Sufis and by practicing Sufi spiritual exercises. At the same time they are anxious to enjoy individual freedom in the Western sense—an attitude that is incompatible with the devotion practiced in Sufism.

Primarily, this incompatibility between the concept of individual freedom in the West and religious devotion, with the disorientation that stems from this, has opened up a new market with many offers for esoteric courses and books which present, under the label of "Sufism," new ways of thinking, and in some cases dubious spiritual cocktails attempting to think Sufism without Islam. And yet there is beauty in this, if such offers result in an increase of yearning for the origin of being.

Who made Sufism (*tasawwuf*) popular in Europe? There are three names to be mentioned: Inayat Khan (1882-1927), G.I. Gurdjieff (1872-1949), and Süleyman Hayati Loras (1904-1985). All three had their share in transmitting a "liberal Sufism" to the world. The interest in Sufism also brought about an interest in well-known Islamic philosophers, whose works underline the universality of Islam. We must consider the varying points of view of Al-Kindi, Al-Farabi, Ibn Sina (Avicenna), Ibn Rushd (Averroes), Sheikh Suhrawardi, Ibn al-Arabi, Mulla Sadra, and that of Al-Ghazali, and note that they all taught under the roof of Islam. So the Europeans take this as a proof for the differences among them and Islam's inclusiveness.

Thanks to the honorable efforts of Süleyman Hayati Loras from Konya it was Mawlana in particular and the ritual of *sama* which became popular when "liberal Sufism" began to spread. But it did not take long until *sama* started to be marketed. There were popular publications, there were advertisements offering spiritual instruction with reference to Mawlana, and there were courses in Mevlevi dance. However, with this obscure market, the demand for an authentic Mevlevi tradition grew as well. There are dependencies of the authentic Mevlevi Order in Switzerland, Germany, and in the Netherlands. The members of these groups come together once a week for prayers, remembrance (*dhikr*), *sama*, and to study. But these

groups also have to deal with contemporary culture and way of thinking, which can become very challenging.

## ISLAMIC CALL TO REASON AND MAWLANA'S MESSAGE

It is important to make clear to Europeans that the Qur'an is not a
"textbook" that can be read with the expectation of owning its knowledge. The revelation of the Qur'an is the miraculous Word of God,
the same One God, Who revealed Torah and the Gospels, correct-
ing the ancient thought about the monotheistic revelation. While
God's revelation aims to touch our hearts and model our being in
order to become His true servants, it calls on us to make good use
of our minds to be guided to the truth. And this approach fits in
perfectly with European perception and thought. A European has
to intellectually discover the enormous potential Islam holds for
our age before he comes to the next step which is the realization of
the truth of Islam. And for this, Mawlana's message is of great help.

Mawlana's impact on Islam of today may be compared with
Einstein's impact on physics. With his theory of relativity Einstein
did not replace Newton's laws, but showed them in a wider context. Mawlana was an ideal lover of our Prophet. He approved plu-
ralism and pointed to the beauty of diversity without disturbing
the essence of Islam. A religious community (*umma*) that does not
approve of diversity falls into fundamentalism. Mawlana proved that
religious faith and democracy can complement each other. Faith in
God requires devotion to the highest authority, i.e. to God and His
commandments. By contrast, living together in a democracy demands
compromises with people who are devoted to other belief systems
or who do not believe in God at all. The answer to this contrast lies
in the acknowledgement of the equality of all people and in the
realization that we are all powerless in front of God.

## MEVLEVI GROUPS TODAY

In the Mevlevi Orders of today there are more and more women.
And it is only natural that they ask for equal rights. They reason
that our Prophet Muhammad (pbuh) fought for the dignity of

women. Thanks to him, the women of his community gained respect.
So it is difficult to accept that women in Islamic countries today enjoy
far fewer rights than men.

As mentioned above, only strong and rational arguments will
enable the Europeans to find their way to the beauty and universality of Islam. Therefore European Mevlevi groups have adopted
philosophical discussions as an important topic. These discussions
do not impair the ability of the members to devote themselves thoroughly to the Divine Spirit, but rather strengthen it. In the end, we
are talking about a competence that I can describe best by presenting some words uttered by a female member of the Mevlevi group
of Switzerland:

> It took me a long time to implement sama in my life. For years
> on end I "only" enjoyed the rotations. But I wished to experi-
> ence the same feeling in my daily routine, too. Every time this
> urging and longing came over me I tried to rotate in spirit and
> to be aware of that memory in my heart. Sama for me is part
> of the so called "doing nothing." The whole universe rotates.
> Being a tiny particle of this universe I leave myself to rotation
> fully aware and in harmony with nature. Sama also shows me
> that I have both feet deep-rooted in this earthly reality. I have
> to be steadfast, persevering, and determined. But at the same
> time I may put forth my hands upwards, show some guts, and
> be free from all questions, attachments, and worldly affairs. I
> may draw a bow between heaven and hell, stay in this world
> and in the other world at the same time, and live in this world
> but do not belong to it, as the dervishes say. Understanding this
> has helped me to return to the point and to find peace in implic-
> it trust in God. It has helped me to become aware that I live in
> a world that is not my real home. While I rotate I can shake off
> the questions that form again and again in my head. It is as if
> they were blown away. In those moments I am just me; I sur-
> render to these moments, and I resemble the flowers, the trees,
> the mountains and the stars in the sky.

Spirituality and religion always refer to systems of faith and experiences which in their totality and universality are not cognizable by
reason and not describable in everyday speech. The corresponding

discourse, however, cannot avoid making use of speech and has to be based on a logic that is understandable and reasonable. Reason is located on a level that is separate from spiritual experience. Therefore, it can only act as a transmitter that tries to describe what was heard in that other world which in dialogue is almost invisible. Mawlana was far more than a poet and far more than a mystic. For the followers of the Mevlevi path he is a holy man whose spirit illuminates the hearts of his followers even today. Mawlana may, with his beauty and universality, touch even rational souls, and thus he may act as a door to Islam.

# RUMI STUDIES IN THE WEST

## Şefik Can

T here is a large audience receptive to Sufism and Rumi, who
is one of the-best selling poets both in the East and the
West. Although the works of Rumi, the lover of humanity
and the lover of God, has now been read by millions of Western
people, very little was known about Rumi and Sufism in the West
until the end of the eighteenth century. Since then, various scholars in the West have made tremendous contributions to the understanding of this remarkable spiritual leader and poet.

Mouradja d'Ohsson's painting of Sama Ceremony:
*Tableau Général de l'Empire Othoman*, 1790

Toward the end of the eighteenth century, a French ambassador named J. de Wallenbourg, who lived in Istanbul for some time,
translated the complete *Masnavi* into French. Unfortunately, there
was a fire in Beyoğlu, Istanbul in 1799, and this important work was
burnt to ashes. Hammer, who was a very well known German orientalist in Turkey and author of *The Ottoman History*, was also
interested in Rumi's work.[1] Indicating the importance of the *Divan-i
Kabir*, Hammer writes:

> By separating from the exoteric differences and world affairs of
> all the positive religions, Rumi found the Supreme and Everlasting
> Being, and on the wings of highest spiritual joys and pleasure,
> he rose to levels that other poets (including Hafiz) could not
> reach. Rumi not only transcends the sun and the moon but also
> time and space, creation, the assembly of *Alast*, and the Judgment
> Day and reaches infinity, and from there he attains the Absolute
> Being that is Everlasting and Everpresent and represents the
> ultimate servant, the infinite love and lover.

Unfortunately, Hammer's translations of the *Masnavi* and the
*Divan-i Kabir* are not as beautiful and eloquent as his translations
of Hafiz. But although these translations did not reflect Rumi's
poetry in its original profundity and taste, they were very important
because they introduced Rumi to the West. Hammer also came to
live in Turkey for some time. It can be said accurately that during his
time in Istanbul, he regularly visited libraries and attended ceremonies
in Mevlevi convents, where he also collected couplets and quatrains
that were recited during these ceremonies. The following couplet is
among these poems that he collected and appears in Rumi's original Persian: "Alas, love, its states and its pain! The fire of love has
burnt my heart."

---

[1]   This valuable scholar, who knew Arabic, Persian, and Turkish very well, translated
the *Divan* by Hafiz of Shiraz into German. In his book *Persian Literature*, published
in 1818, Hammer discusses Rumi's works extensively (pages 163-98) and describes
the Honorable *Masnavi* as a book that should be read by all Sufis from the Ganges
River to the shores of the Bosphorous.

In those years the odes of Friedrich Ruckert (d. 1866) were published in Germany. These odes all expressed divine love. Ruckert, who is regarded as the most well-known German orientalist, tried to introduce the divine love that Rumi expressed in his poems to the Germans by employing the ode form for the first time in Germany. In fact, Friedrich Ruckert was not only a great German orientalist but also a great Sufi. With the encouragement and help of Hammer, he learned Arabic, Persian, and Turkish. He was a lover of God in spirit. He fell in love with Rumi after reading the honorable *Masnavi* and the *Divan-i Kabir*. He found himself in Rumi. He translated forty-four of Rumi's odes into German verse. He published these translations that he composed with love and feeling, their deep meanings in his heart, in Stuttgart in 1820 under the title *Odes*. After two years, Ruckert's selections were published in Leipzig under the title *Östliche Rosen* (Eastern Roses). Afterwards he translated in verse form poets like Sa'di, Hafiz, and Jami. With his work, Ruckert wanted to show Europeans the greatness of the Sufis of Islam and make them feel the divine love that these Sufis express. In order to have an idea about the translations that this great poet and Sufi composed, I am presenting the poem "The Rose" selected from the *Divan-i Kabir* and translated into German with its original. This poem smells of roses:

> Today is a spring day, a day of joy and happiness. This year where the roses bloom more than usual is the year of the roses...
>
> Help has arrived from beyond, from the rose garden of the friend's face. Therefore, our eyes won't see the rose wither and its leaves falling.
>
> Everybody's eyes are in awe before the rose's beauty, elegance, magnificence, color, and smell. In the garden it is smiling with its beautiful mouth. It is whispering the secrets of the nightingale's love and the virtues of the rose into the ear of the cypress tree...
>
> The rose is so graceful, so elegant that the world of dreams is too narrow to dream of the rose.
>
> Who is meant by "the rose"? A messenger from the garden of the intellect, from the grove of spirit. What is "the rose"? A

document that describes the beauty and the highness of the rose of truth that neither turns brown nor withers.

Let us hold onto the rose's skirt and be its fellow traveler so that we may journey happily to the origin of the rose, the everlasting rose shoot.

The origin of the rose, the everlasting rose shoot, has sprung from the sweat of Mustafa, peace and blessings be upon him, and has grown from His grace.

Thanks to that Gracious Being, it turned from a crescent to a full moon. You may pluck the rose's leaves and break its branches and yet they grant it a new spirit, a new life, they bestow it with hands and wings.

See how the rose has answered the invitation of the spring. Just like Abraham's, the Friend of God, four pigeons that were resurrected after being killed and returned to their master.

O Mawlana, be silent! Don't open your lips. Sit in the rose's shadow and just like the rosebud, secretly smile with your lips.[2]

Through Ruckert's odes, Rumi became known in Germany, and with this book the ode form entered German literature. Soon, another German translation of *Divan-i Shams-i Tabrizi*, which contains selected poems from Rumi's *Divan-i Kabir*, appeared. Toward the end of the last century scholars and intellectuals all over the world have begun to show interest in Rumi and his works. In one of his books, *Ethe*, a famous German orientalist described Rumi as "the greatest Sufi poet of the East and at the time." In Germany, Rumi's work has been studied extensively by Helmut Ritter, who also is very well known in Turkey. This great scholar produced very valuable studies about Rumi's life, poetry, the reed flute, and whirling ceremonies that were based on the oldest manuscripts. With his studies on the history of Sufism, he helped us to understand better many aspects of Rumi. One also should not forget the great poet and lover of Rumi, Hans Meinke (d. 1974), who was influenced very much by Rumi. Meinke, who first got to know Rumi through the works of German orientalists, was fascinated by the Divine Love in Rumi and

---

[2]  Rumi, *Divan-i Kabir*, vol. III, no. 1348.

dedicated all his poetry to Rumi. He also traveled to Konya to visit Rumi's tomb. Although this poet did not know Persian, he felt Rumi's spirit and especially the infinite Divine Love in Rumi's poems and reflected it surprisingly well in the hundred odes that he wrote in Rumi's name. As an example, I am presenting one of his poems as it appears translated from German by Mehmet Önder:

> O Rumi, since I became you,
> The turmoil stopped . . .
> O Rumi, since I became you,
> North has become south and south has become north.
> One pole has created the other pole.
> Chaos has melted in harmony.
> At the shore of the pulsating sea,
> Tell me if there has remained any silent gulf.
> Tell me if in your sight,
> Has there remained any meaningless word?
> Is there a man who doesn't dance?
> O Rumi, I am the center of the circle of the heavens,
> Till I became you.

We also should remember the famous orientalist and an admirer of Rumi, Prof. Annemarie Schimmel with respect.[3] Of the orientalists in the West, Schimmel has written the largest number of books and articles about Rumi. She not only has written about Rumi in German, English, and Turkish but also has translated Iqbal's *Jawidnama* into Turkish and has written a commentary on it.

---

3    Schimmel (d. 2003), who was also poet, was born in Erfurt, Germany in 1922. She showed interest in Arabic early in her youth, and in addition to Arabic she also learned Persian and Turkish. After graduating from Berlin University at age 19, Schimmel fell in love with Rumi, reading his poetry in its original language. She began translating Rumi's poetry. She came to Turkey for the first time in 1952 and lectured in Ankara University's Department of History of Religions in the School of Theology for five years. Afterward she joined Bonn University. In 1967, she began lecturing at Harvard University. Many universities awarded her honorary doctorate degrees. Her book on Rumi is *The Triumphal Sun: A Study of the Works of Jalaluddin* Rumi (Albany, NY: State University of New York Press, 1993).

Just as different people understand and value Rumi according to their own personal views, talents, inclinations, perceptions, and thoughts, different nations have approached Rumi in their own ways. A careful study will show that among all European nations, the Germans and the British are the nations that have concentrated most on Rumi. The disciplined, hard working, skillful German nation has at the same time a mystical spirit. For example, Martin Luther (d. 1546), who began the Reformation, is a German. Since Germans are inclined to faith and religion in spirit, they have identified themselves with Rumi and have worked on Rumi's books more than any other nation in Europe, except for the British.

As far as the British interest in Rumi, Hippolyte Taine (d. 1893), an expert in English literature, maintained that the inhabitants of the British Isles, which are separated geographically from continental Europe and surrounded with thick fog and high waves, were not content with their surroundings and feeling the urge to open up to the outside world, they sought out something overseas. Unlike the French who are theoretical and Italians who are artistic and ponderous in nature, the determined and pragmatic British also have a strong inclination toward mystical thought. Their love of experimentation, dislike of concepts imposed on them, and more logical approach to emotions have lead the British to understand Rumi more deeply and study him thoroughly.

We shall end this section with the British admirers of Rumi. In 1881, Sir James W. Redhouse translated in verse the first volume of the *Masnavi* into English. He also included a number of stories from Aflaki's *Manaqibu'l-Arifin* at the beginning of his translation. E.H. Whinfield studied all six volumes of the *Masnavi*. He then translated in verse selected passages and published them in 1898 under the name *Masnavi-i Manavi*. In his shortened *Masnavi* in verse, Whinfield summarized the stories and then diligently translated into English the portions about spiritual matters in rhyme and meter. The fact that this *Masnavi* translation was republished twice in 1979 and 1984 shows how positively this translation was received. In 1898, in the foreword of the first edition, E. H. Whinfield introduced the *Masnavi* to the English readers, writing: "The *Masnavi* addresses those who leave the world, try to know and to be with God, efface their selves and devote themselves to spiritual contemplation."

E. H. Palmer, who is known in England for his remarkable studies in Sufism, published selected poems of Rumi in a work titled *Song of the Reed*. With this publication, Rumi was introduced not only to the British audience but also to all the people in the English speaking world. In a periodical published in 1886, a scholar named J. Scherr wrote about Rumi: "I swear that there has appeared no lover of God sweeter and more charming than Rumi in the world." R. A. Nicholson, regarded as one of the greatest orientalists and Rumi scholars, produced his first work on Rumi with the translation of a number of selected poems. In this book titled *Selected Poems from the Divan-i Shams-i Tabriz* there are forty-eight poems selected from the *Divan-i Kabir*. The original text of each ode is included in the book as well as its translation, which is placed on the following page. There are also explanations at the end of this book. One should confess the fact that in Turkey, there is no Rumi anthology published that is as well prepared, as tastefully and carefully selected, nor as inclusive of the original text.

One also should note that the previously mentioned orientalists—the British scholar Graham, the German orientalist Hammer, and the German Sufi poet Ruckert—declared that all the poems in the copies of the *Divan-i Shams-i Tabrizi* and *Divan-i Shamsu'l-Haqa'iq* to which they had access were authentic poems by Rumi. Since the edition of the *Divan-i Kabir* that was put together carefully by the Tehran University Professor Furuzanfar and published in Tehran did not exist at that time, these works that contain poems that do not belong to Rumi have misled Western orientalists.

This great lover of Rumi worked all his life and with Rumi's inspiration and spiritual influence translated many invaluable works of other Sufis and other poets into English and showed the path to many people with a taste for gnosis. But the most important work of Nicholson is the translation of and commentary on the six volumes of the *Masnavi*. In this work that was published in eight volumes beginning in 1925, Nicholson produced the *Masnavi*'s most reliable text as well as its translation and commentary. Nicholson was not only a great orientalist and a renowned scholar but also a great lover of God. As related by his friends and students, he would shed tears during *Masnavi* lectures, becoming enraptured. In a room of his house decorated in oriental fashion, he would prepare the explanation of the *Masnavi* dressed in clothing wearing the long, round Mevlevi hat on his head. It is said that Nicholson completed this commentary in forty years.

A. J. Arberry who headed the Oriental Languages Department at Cambridge University after Nicholson, followed the same path as his predecessor and continued to translate Rumi's works into English. In addition to translating Rumi's quatrains and *Fihi Ma fihi* into English, he also published a selection of tales from the *Masnavi* in two volumes. A few years prior to his death, Arberry said to a close friend: "I will devote the remaining years of my life exclusively to study Rumi's work because it is possible to find spiritual cures and consolation for the miseries of our time in it."

I also should quote these sentences from a speech by E. W. F. Tomlin, former chairman of the Turkish-English Cultural Committee, that he delivered at the memorial celebrations for Rumi in 1960: "In spite of the elevation of Rumi's thought there is also a phenomenon called concrete imagination. This infiltrates the reader's spirit and attracts him to itself. Whenever I read passages from Rumi, it reminds me of Chaucer. But Chaucer (d. 1400), who is one of the most distinguished personalities of English literature, does not have religious views as deep as those of Rumi. One cannot reach the truth immediately. As Rumi says in the first book of the *Masnavi* 'God has set up a ladder in front of us. We have to climb it step by step.' I find the truth that Rumi has brought not only to his home country but also to us all in the fourth book of his *Masnavi*: 'The believers are many but men are one.' I will conclude my speech with a quote from Rumi that points to the same truth and is an example of the above-mentioned concrete imagination: 'The sunlight from the sky is thousand-fold with respect to the courtyards that it illuminates. But if you remove the walls from in between, all these fragmented lights are one and the same thing."'

Perhaps not as much as the British and the German, the French also showed interest in Rumi. Some French explorers who traveled through the Ottoman Empire were very interested in the whirling ceremonies in the Mevlevi lodges. They had included these ceremonies in their memoirs, and some painters painted whirling dervishes, which increased this interest. C. L. Huart, a French orientalist who visited Konya in 1897, wrote a book on Konya. He later translated Aflaki's *Manaqibu'l-Arifin* into French under the title *Whirling Dervishes*. This translation led Maurice Barres, a famous literary figure and a French Academy member, to visit Konya. Barres, who visited Rumi's lodge and shrine in Konya in 1919, took notes which in 1923 he published under the title *An Interview in the Eastern Countries*. Mehmet Önder translated some sections from this book in 1969 under the name *In the Presence of Rumi*.

Maurice Barres, this lover of Rumi, begins his memoirs as follows:

> I can't wait. I want to see Rumi's lodge, whirling hall and shrine, experience his Divine rapture and hear the melodies of his poetry. He is such a genius that odor, light, music, and a little bit of bohemianism emanate from him. His original expressions in the poetry are vivid and divine. It enraptures the reader. Only the reader? No. Jalaladdin Rumi himself is in rapture and whirling in his poems. He placed a book in our hands so as to draw us into his magical atmosphere. If I am fortunate I will see the Mevlevi dervishes, the followers of his path, who very proficiently perform his music. His memory has been living for seven hundred years from generation to generation, and his name is mentioned around his tomb more enthusiastically every day. How fortunate am I![4]

From Asaf Halet Çelebi's translation of the same book, Barres confesses: "In my opinion, the life of no poet, whom I consider to be

---

[4]    Mehmet Önder, *Hazret-i Mevlana Hayatı ve Eserleri* ("Life and Works of Rumi"), Istanbul: Tercüman Yayınları, p. 232.

the messengers of the world of enthusiasm, light, and joy, compares
to the life of Rumi. After seeing the dervishes whirling and singing
to his rhythm I noticed that there is something lacking in Dante,
Shakespeare, Goethe, and Hugo."[5] Barres' book received much
attention in France and many French scholars, literary personalities, and poets were introduced to Rumi. Also Mme Myriam Harry
published a book entitled *Mevlana Jalalu'd-deen* in 1956. Today in
Paris Prof. Eva de Vitray has been studying Rumi and his works, and
has completed a work titled *Rumi and Sufism*.[6] Prof. Irene Melikoff,
a lover of Rumi, also works in this area.

In Italy, too, there are admirers of Rumi. We must remember the
Rome University Professors Alessander Bausani and Anna Masala.
In Holland, Prof. Brakell Busy and Dr. Carp, in Denmark, Prof.
Asmussen, and in Switzerland, Prof. Burgel, all are among the admir-
ers of Rumi. In recent years there is increasing interest in Rumi in
Russia. The broad research done in 1972 by Radi Fis in Moscow on
Rumi's life, views, and books is an example of this interest.

In the United Stated there is great admiration for Rumi. He
deserves the title of the most read poet in America. His influence
is evident in academia as well as Sufi circles. There are many names
who have written on Rumi. William Chittick, Kabir Helminski,
Colman Barks, and recently Franklin Lewis are some examples. Also,
there are institutions dedicated to the teachings of Rumi.[7]

---

5   Asaf Halet Çelebi, *Mevlana Hayatı ve Şahsiyeti*, ("The life and personality of Rumi"),
    Istanbul, Kanaat Kitabevi, 1939:50.
6   Eva de Vitray-Meyerovitch, *Rumi and Sufism* (Sausalito, CA: Post-Apollo Press,
    1977 [French]; 1987 [English Translation]).
7   The Washington based "Rumi Forum for Interfaith Dialogue" is one of them. There
    is also an annual Rumi Festival held in North Carolina.

# EVA DE VITRAY MEYEROVITCH AND HER CONTRIBUTIONS TO THE PROMOTION OF RUMI

Abdullah Öztürk

J ust like rivers that reach the ocean after traversing various continents and tracks, Eva de Vitray Meyerovitch, who encountered Rumi after having encountered many religions and languages, incessantly persisted in understanding the thought of Rumi and then elucidating and sustaining it. This feature of her is what makes her different from the others. Meyerovitch, who worked on Rumi for her doctoral thesis and translated, for the first time, many of his works into French, attracted the attention of the West with her introduction, "La quète de l'absolu" (The Quest for the Absolute), to the *Masnavi* translation. In her introduction, Meyerovitch maintains that the *Masnavi* included information on theories of nuclear physics, which did not see the actual day of light until the 1940s, and that one would face enormous difficulty in attempting to throw a light on Rumi's relationship with this nuclear force, as it has nothing to do with Democritus, nor Islamic philosophy, nor was it known in the time of Rumi or the ensuing periods.[1] Ms. Meyerovitch—who came to be called Hawwa after her embracing of Islam—presented Rumi's understanding of Islam and Sufism in refutation of those striving to misrepresent the religion in the West, as well as lending her precious support to the establishment and subsequent activities of many organizations in Paris, like Islam et Occident and Soufisme d'Orient et d'Occident. An administrator and expert researcher at the French Scientific Research Center (CNRS), and a

---

[1]  *Masnavi* translation, pg.11; VI/4580, 38, 2900; II/1706, 1611; VI/3850.

lecturer of philosophy at al-Azhar and other universities in Egypt, Ms. Meyerovitch additionally received the title, "Docteur Honoris Causa" from Selçuk University in 1987, for the invaluable services rendered to Rumi and Turkish Culture. Having embraced Rumi, in her words, as "the greatest mystic genius of all time, my spiritual leader," and owing to her humble yet elevated intellectual status in Rumi thought, Eva de Vitray thus paved the way for many Westerners and Easterners alike to accept Islam, just like she herself had done.

EVA DE VITRAY'S ENCOUNTER WITH RUMI

There are, in life, such messages and signs, which we sometimes see, sometimes live, and at other times experience—while, on occasions, none of the foregoing take place. There are also messages of another kind, enshrouded in flesh and bones, visible in the form of man, or aligned on pages like pearls. Our familiarity with these messages emerge at unexpected times and places and may initially begin as an ostensible coincidence, then continue with awe, and finally conclude with a realization of wisdom and truth.

The meeting between Rumi and Eva de Vitray Meyerovitch, a researcher, writer on philosophy, and translator, born into an acclaimed family of French aristocrats in 1909, in the region of Boulogne, France, was actualized with a message of the kind just explained. Eva de Vitray later described this rather interesting, astonishing, and— inasmuch as its consequences are concerned—thought-provoking meeting, at her residence in Paris at number 75, Claude Bernard Street, in 1975, in a setting which also included the presence of a French television crew.[2]

> One day, searching through the library of the Sorbonne University, I happened to come across an essay of half a page on the thought of Rumi written by Dr. Muhammad Iqbal. After reading this text, comprising a short message of Rumi's, I became confounded, stranded amid a dilemma, in that either Rumi was speaking the truth, or Greek philosophy, which I had been

---

[2]    Eva de Vitray Meyerovitch, *L'islam, l'autre visage.*

immersed in until that time. Thus my first task was to hunt for
works on Rumi, but to no avail, as I could not find, in the entire
collection of the library, another record pertaining to Rumi.
The only thing I could do in dispersing my curiosity on the
subject was to get in touch with Rumi through Dr. Muhammad
Iqbal, which indeed I did.[3]

As regards the reason behind the enormous impression left on
Eva by the Rumi meeting, an experience she explained to her friends
each time with excitement, the answer is twofold, of which one is
her past years of education and work in the West, while the other
is the predominant notion of metaphysics upheld by the modern
world and the crisis connected with it.

Having completed her primary education in a Catholic school,
Meyerovitch continued her schooling by graduating from the lyceum
with certificates in Latin and Greek, followed by an entrance into
and subsequent graduation from the Faculty of Law. During the
outbreak of World War II, she assumed her position as an expert
researcher in the Scientific Research Center in Paris. In the mean-
time, she devoted herself to studying certain problems of Catholicism,
a research which led to, in due course, extensive religious and philosophical investigations.[4]

As also attested to by Collette-Nour Brahy, in the commencing years of scientific research, Eva de Vitray was an exceptional
researcher seeing to vast scientific areas such as history, law, divini-
ty, psychology, and philosophy—and conversant in Greek, Latin,
English and French—who was moreover profoundly skilled in scientifically sifting data accumulated from the interactions between
numerous disciplines.[5]

---

3    Eva de Vitray, *Konya et la danse cosmique*. Translated into Turkish by A.Öztürk, *Konya
     ve Sema*, Republic of Turkey, Governorship of Konya, Office of Culture, 2000, 13.
4    ibid., p.13.
5    Colette-Nour Brahy: 'A l'écoute de l'essentiel', the international conference organ-
     ized by "l'association terres d'Europe," under the aegis of Unesco/Paris, 12-13 January,
     2000.

By now Eva, who was also an expert on Plato, was adamant, just like her contemporary, Roger Garaudy, that insofar as human values were concerned, the modern world was edging towards an ominous crisis. As indicated by Garaudy, with the dry acceptance of reason as the sole guide in the hapless bid to establish the sovereignty of man over God, the post-Renaissance philosophers became intoxicated with an insatiable appetite to exploit other continents and peoples, and with the power accrued from science and technology, to become masters of nature. The remainder of hope attached to the realization of this fancy, however, diminished entirely with the outbreak of both World Wars.

To ascertain the cause behind Eva de Vitray Meyerovitch's inclination towards religious searches and remedies following World War II, it would be wise to recall some key statements attributed to French philosophers:

> The despair of the modern man, who first murdered the deity and then purged all feelings of divine from within him, forced him toward the rebellious literature of masters like Heidegger, Sartre and Foucault.[6]

In turn, Jean Paul Sartre, who found himself amid that very depression in 1942, stated the following in his, *L'être et le néant* (Being and Nothingness):

> Man is a being with the pretension to be God. (...) But the idea of God is contradictory. We're wasting time for nothing, "Man is a meaningless passion."[7]

In similar vein, the existentialist writer, Albert Camus, asserted that, "Life is nonsense; it has no meaning"[8] in his *L'homme révolté* (The Rebellious Man). Again, another French writer, Andre Malraux,

---

6   Roger Garaudy, *Avons-nous besoin de Dieu?* Declée Brouwer, 1993, 16-39.
7   J.Paul Sartre, *L'être et le néant*, 653-708.
8   Albert Camus, *L'homme revolté*.

confessed, "Our civilization was the first to ask the question 'Does life have a meaning?' which, again, she answered 'I don't know.'"[9]

Precisely aware of this approach, that by the expedient of refuting the "universal mind," humanity had nailed shut its own coffin, so to speak, and while searching for a solution to the crisis of modern man in early Christian texts, Eva de Vitray Meyerovitch fell upon a short text of Rumi's, an unexpected meeting which, by her own account, altered the flow and direction of her life.

Busy searching for the source of Rumi's thought, Ms. Meyerovitch followed the track of Dr. Iqbal—the Muslim scholar who was instrumental in articulating the formation of Pakistan—initially coming across his English work, *The Reconstruction of Religious Thought in Islam*, a book which addressed most of her queries while also presenting to her the universality of Islam. Thus having acquired a preliminary exposure to Islam through Rumi's interpretation, she then became conversant in the subject through the scholarship of Iqbal, as she contemplated embracing Islam. She again elucidates, the decision-making process herself, which in terms of her surroundings, position, and family status was by no means an easy task:

> This would have been a simple and wonderful thing, if one were a disciple by the side of Rumi. (...) But my first steps towards Islam, after having read Iqbal, were not easy, having been reared by a Catholic grandmother and married to a Jew. Suffering from the lack of a guide, I would sometimes lose control, feeling, as if crazy, if I were to realize such a decision. One day I prayed, imploring, "O God! Please tell me what I should do. Send me a sign!" That sign came with a dream, in which I had been buried in a grave carrying a gravestone with the name, "Hawwa," written in Arabic. This seemed to me quite peculiar, enhanced by the fact that, in my dream, I was wondering how I could be buried and at the same time see my own gravestone. When I woke up, I recalled the utterance in my dream of these words, "All right, dear, you insisted on a sign, and that sign is this: You will be buried as a Muslim." Consequently, I continued my life journey as a Muslim. Fifteen years later, I conducted my first visit to

---

9    Garaudy, ibid, 6.

Istanbul. A dervish, whom I had previously known at UNESCO, took me for a tour in the *Samahana*, which at the time was undergoing renovation. During the visit, I froze for a moment, in complete surprise, as I saw a grave tremendously resembling the grave I had seen years ago in my dream. When I inquired of guide Halil Can as to what it was, he informed me that it was a cemetery belonging to *Mevlevi* women, a message which simultaneously awakened in me the necessity of becoming a *Mevlevi* myself.[10]

While explaining the dream, additionally cited in her book *Islam, l'autre visage* (The Other Face of Islam), to her friends, Ms. Meyerovitch occasionally slipped in a joke, asserting, "I made a wish in French and received a reply in French and Arabic, from which I understand that God knows French as well."

Thus having met Rumi and become acquainted with Islam, Ms. Meyerovitch's greatest desire and toil had now become that of promoting the works of Rumi to the world to illumine the road to the Truth. A lecturer of philosophy at al-Azhar in Egypt for six years, as a member of the Scientific Research Center in France, she was well conversant with the West as well as the Islamic world, and she was profoundly convinced that authentic Islam could only be presented to the West through the teachings and philosophy of Rumi.

Corresponding with this aim, in an international congress, she explicitly avowed, "What I wish to do is to identify Rumi's messages, which have preserved their prevalence, and present them to Western youth who are deprived of spirituality and thirsty for meaning."[11]

Deciding on this path, she vowed to learn Persian, subsequently studying it for three years, staying for a period in Iran. Coincidentally, during this time, she associated with the former dean of Tabriz University, Jamshid Mortazavi, from whom she received a promise of jointly translating the *Masnavi* into French, an ideal realized soon after.

---

10 Eva de Vitray Meyerovitch, *L'islam, l'autre visage*, Le seuil, 1995, 55-56 and 77.

11 Eva de Vitray Meyerovitch, "1st International Rumi Congress" 3-5 May 1987, Konya, 27.

THE CONTRIBUTION OF MS. MEYEROVITCH
TO THE PROMOTION OF RUMI

Eva de Vitray Meyerovitch authored or edited almost thirty works, and her contribution to the study and promotion of Rumi can be encapsulated under five points.

1- Translated Rumi's works into French for the first time, along with the striking scientific commentary she offered in the presentation of these works.

2- Authored books based on research, for the purposes of promoting Rumi.

3- Presented papers pertaining to Rumi at international meetings and congresses.

4- Contributed to establishing organizations such as Islam et Occident (Islam and the West) and Soufisme d'Orient et d'Occident (Sufism in the East and West), whose scientific activities can still be seen via the Internet, and through which the thoughts of Rumi are promulgated.

5- The activities she bequeathed after her death, and messages posted on the Internet by the youth she had reared with the love of Rumi.

Her leading works of translation from Persian to French pertaining to Rumi and the *Mevlevi Sufism* are as follows:

- *Odes mystiques* (Mystical Odes), Editions Klingsieck, 1973 (Selections from the *Diwan-i Kabir*).
- *Le livre du dedans* (The Book of the Inside), de Djalal-od-Din Rumi, Editions Sinbad, 1976.
- *La parole secrète de Sultan Valad* (The Secret Words of Sultan Walad), Editions du Rocher, 1982.
- *Rubaiy'at*, Editions Albin Michel, 1987.
- *Lettres de Rumi* (Rumi's Letters), Editions J. Renard, 1990.
- *Mathnawi de Djalal-od-Din Rumi*, 6 vol (506000 vers) Editions Rocher, 1990.

- *Maitre et disciple* (Master and Disciple) (Sultan Walad Marif) Paris, 1982, Edition Sinbad.

In addition, her own written works on Rumi and Sufism include the following:

- *Mystique et poésie en islam* (Mysticism and Poetry in Islam), Editions Desclee de Brovwer, 1972.
- *Les chemins de la lumière* (The Paths of Light), Contes sufis, Editions RETZ, 1982.
- *Rumi et le soufisme* (Rumi and Sufism), ed. Sinbad, 1978.
- *Konya et la danse cosmique* (Konya and the Cosmic Dance), ed. Jacqueline Renard, 1989.

As is evident from the list provided, Eva de Vitray Meyerovitch effectively concentrated her attention solely on Rumi after learning Persian, and especially after 1970, whereupon she undertook a great volume of publishing to promote Rumi in the West, including translations of Rumi's works from Persian to French, and specific research and writing projects which enunciated the principles of Sufism and the works of Rumi. In actual fact, the translations and research published between 1972 and 1990 are works that complete one another in the process of elaborating Rumi's thought. In particular, her *Mystique et poésie en islam* (Poetry and Mysticism in Islam), and *Djalal-ud-din Rumi et l'ordre de derviches tourneurs* (Mawlana Jalaladdin Rumi and the Whirling Dervishes), published in 1972, evoked enormous feedback from the arena of literature and poetry, whereby Western readers, captivated by the texts, thus began to delve further into the *Masnavi* and other works of Rumi, as her publications were so filled with various examples extracted from the extant legacy of Rumi. Thus, Western readers became aware of the fact that Rumi was not only the sheikh of whirling dervishes, but also the man behind such elegantly composed literature, and one of the primary narrators of universal thought and symbolism.

In *Rumi et le soufisme* (Rumi and Sufism), made available in 1977 in French and subsequently translated into many other Western languages, she presents a short biography of Rumi's family, their trials and tribulations, their journey to Anatolia, the time and reason of their settlement in Konya, the birth of the *Mevlevi Sufism*, and its historical spread into the Balkans.

Following this train of thought, she describes in her book, *Konya et la danse cosmique* (Konya and the Cosmic Dance),[12] published in 1989, that the tomb of Rumi is situated in Konya, known previously as Iconium, a capital city for the Romans and the Seljuk Turks, which also happens to be located only 40 km away from the world's oldest known residence, the 9000-year-old Çatalhöyük; further, she aptly reminds readers that it was also in this very area that St. Paul commenced preaching the Bible, and then she uses all of this information to entice her Western friends to take part in the Shab-i Arus Ceremony held annually at Konya. The book, which also describes Yunus Emre and his poetry, is essentially a cultural history of Konya.

In brief, just like rivers that reach the ocean after traversing various continents and tracks, Eva de Vitray Hawwa Meyerovitch, who encountered Rumi after having encountered many religions and languages, incessantly persisted in understanding the thought of Rumi, and then in elucidating and sustaining it. With her humble yet elevated intellectual status in Rumi thought, Eva de Vitray paved the way for many Westerners and Easterners alike to accept Islam, just like she did herself. Her uniqueness is precisely that. Having already embraced Rumi as the greatest mystic genius of all time and her only leader, she expressed a final wish during her doctoral acceptance speech at Selçuk University, in 1987. The desire of this altruistic soul, who had devoted the greater part of her life to Rumi, was to be buried in a cemetery behind the tomb of Rumi, whom she intensely esteemed. Owing to her age and ill-health, as well as to the non-existence of a written will in relation to this, however, her wish was unfortunately never realized. It could be, perhaps, that her two sons never gave their consent to the fulfillment of

---

[12]  Eva de Vitray, *Konya et la danse cosmique*. Translated into Turkish by A. Özturk, *Konya ve Sema*, Republic of Turkey, Governorship of Konya, Office of Culture 2000.

the wish, but on this matter, we possess no conclusive knowledge. What we do know for certain, though, is that she is currently at rest in a Muslim cemetery near Paris without even a headstone bearing her name. We earnestly hope for God's boundless compassion on the soul of Eva de Vitray Hawwa Meyerovitch, who, through her tireless work, will never cease to be with us and to be a hope for the countless souls to whom she set her life to guide.

# PART IV

---

## Rumi Poetry

# The Song of the Reed

Listen to this reed-flute, how it is wistfully singing!
About separation, it is complaining:

఩ ఙ

"Ever since I was uprooted from the reed-bed,
All eyes gazing upon my cry shed tears that never dried.

఩ ఙ

"I want a bosom torn, torn from separation,
So that I may share the pain of lamentation:

఩ ఙ

"Whoever has been parted from his origin,
Yearns always for the moment of reunion.

఩ ఙ

"In every company, I moaned and cried,
The miserable and the happy, both in friendship tried.

఩ ఙ

"Each became friendly with me according to their fancy,
Yet none sought to discover the secrets deep within me.

఩ ఙ

"Though my secret is in the notes I wail,
The senses are unable to unveil,

఩ ఙ

"Body from soul, and soul from body, are not concealed,
Yet to no mortal eye is ever the soul revealed."

఩ ఙ

Tis the fervor of love in the reed's wailing blow, not mere hot air,
May he be naught if he be lacking this fervent desire for fire.

఩ ఙ

It's the flames of love in this reed-flute burning,
It's the ferment of love in this wine enrapturing.

ಹ ೕ

The reed-flute is the confidant of all parted from the beloved,
Its wailing tones shred the shrouds of hearts deeply covered.

ಹ ೕ

Who saw like the reed-flute in grief yet with the cure in its pain?
Who saw like the reed-flute, a longing lover and a true companion?

ಹ ೕ

The reed-flute sings of the way stained with blood
It tells of the beloved for whom Majnun's heart bled.

ಹ ೕ

None but the crazed lover can truly have a say to hear,
For the wise tongue carries away only the lowly ear.

ಹ ೕ

Reunion is held up as the days grow, lengthening,
Nights pull together with blazing suffering.

ಹ ೕ

Who cares for painful days now gone
For You remain, O You Pure One!

ಹ ೕ

Only the fish drowning in water grow thirstier,
Yet the days of those with no share grow longer

ಹ ೕ

This reed's ecstatic state of love to the ripe is all comprehensible,
But beyond the grasp of the raw, to whom my only word's farewell!

*Rumi, Masnavi, Vol. I, 1-18, translated by Hüseyin Bingül*

# Musical Notation of the Third Salute of the Sama Ceremony

From the third salute of the Sama ceremony, which is the transformation of rapture into love, and therefore the complete submission of the lover to the Beloved. This third salute is called, *"Panjgâh Âyín-i Sharíf,"* one of the oldest Turkish musical compositions of the Sama ceremony. The lyric of the opening three couplets of Rumi's *"The Song of the Reed"* is set to music by an unknown Mevlevi composer and is also known as *"Basta-i Qadim,"* meaning "Ancient Composition."

# ECSTASY IN THE SONG OF
# THE REED'S PLAINTIVE NOTES

Hüseyin Bingül

R umi expresses his burning love in the form of linked stories throughout his *Masnavi*, which is an enormous poetic work in six large volumes, all of it written in couplets.
In "the Song of the Reed," the first story of his masterpiece, the
poetic genius pours his own heart out, utilizing the reed-flute as it
complains of separation from the reed-bed. The central metaphor
of the reed-flute is that of longing, and its song symbolizes the music
of Rumi's own heart burning with love and yearning; it always longs
for the Beloved and sings like the reed-flute. Rumi, the poet of lovers,
experiences separation and company, sorrow and rejoicing, all together at the same time, and he is wishful to share the flood of the ecstasies
of his own heart for the Beloved in the song of the reed's plaintive
notes.

In relation to the story of the reed singing wistfully, Türkmen
recommends that the reader submit to the spiritual illumination Rumi
offers at the beginning of his masterpiece in the first eighteen couplets, rightfully putting forward the idea that the story is, "like an
entrance to his great villa, where he welcomes his guests and gives
them the keys of the rooms, without which the guests might get lost
and falter in the corridors of his grand villa—the *Masnavi*."[1]

While Rumi is asking for the audience to "*listen to this reed-
flute*," in the opening line, he never seems to talk directly to the audience; rather, using his great ability as a teacher and poet, he attracts

---

[1]    Türkmen, Erkan, *The Essence of Rumi's Masnavi*, 1992:63, Konya: Misket Ltd.

the audience's attention to the song of the reed instead. In doing so, the great saint-poet manifests a lover's extraordinary yearning to meet with the Beloved through the song of the reed, whose plaintive tunes become an allegory for the soul's sorrow at being separated from the Creator and sent to this world.

## RUMI'S INTERPRETATION OF JOURNEYING TO THE WORLD

Utilizing the reed-flute, Rumi breathes his own soul and understanding into people through the song of the reed and draws our attention to the Sufi understanding that this world is the realm of separation because our spirit is not corporeal and, therefore, does not belong to this material world, where God acts behind the "veil of cause and effect." Rather, the human spirit belongs to the immaterial, metaphysical worlds, where we can, and will, have truer and more comprehensive knowledge and experience about the Divine reality.

Rumi takes the spiritually attentive reader far back in time, to the creation of humankind, through the story of the reed being parted from the *"reed-bed,"* with all the finger-holes carved into it, and the natural hollow it has for the Flutist to breathe life into the dry substrate:

> And remember when your Lord said to the angels:
> "I am creating a mortal from dried, sounding clay, from molded dark mud. When I have fashioned him in due proportions and breathed into him of My spirit..." (Hijr 15:28-29)

Rumi refers to the Qur'anic verses above using the analogy of the reed, by which he effectively reveals, in a very condensed form, the relationship between God and His human creation: Journeying *from God*, we are sent to this transitory world to journey *back towards and in God* – through the manifestations of the Divine Attributes and Names—annihilating our egos *in the Divine Will* by setting our hearts wholly *on God*, and hopefully guiding others, as Rumi himself does, on the same journey *in the way of God*. Being well-aware of our subsistence and permanence *by and with God*, Rumi awakens us in the traveling *toward God* by following a Sufi way of spiritual training, until we reach the recognition *of God* and possess *knowledge and love of God.*

## THE COVENANT AND THE DIVINE TRUST

Rumi's central metaphor, the reed-flute, is torn from the "reed-bed," which is a symbol for the original source of the spirit when it existed in the Presence of God. Before we came to exist in this transitory world, our spirits dwelt in some other world, which Rumi calls the "World of Spirit."[2] Rumi refers to the "pledge of faith," whose seal all men and women carry in their spirits—spirits that have been burdened by the Divine Trust in the World of Spirit, and then sent to this fleeting world to pass through various tests and obstacles set along their way:

> And remember when your Lord brought forth from the children of Adam, from their reins, their seed, and made them testify of themselves, (saying): "Am I not your Lord?" They said: "Yes, assuredly. We testify!" (A'raf 7:172)

The reed's parting from its source alludes to the spirit's being sent to the corporeal world and its imprisonment in the corporeal body, as it tries to free itself from its shackles and chains. Before the day of reunion with its Creator, and the attainment of the utmost proximity with the Beloved after death, the self can free itself from this prison of the body, as Rumi says, with the ladder of love placed in front of it: "Since the day you came to this world of being, a ladder has been placed before you so that you may escape."[3]

After humankind's ready acceptance of the Trust and their being sent to the world, human beings recollect the meaning of their affirmative answer to the question the Creator poses—while some people seem to forget their pledge, in opposition to their conscience, and resist submitting their egos to the Real Self. This Divine Trust in the human soul, however, is endowed to be kept in the best way

---

[2]    See Can, Şefik, *Fundamentals of Rumi's Thought*, 2005: 270, NJ: The Light Inc.
[3]    See Can, Ibid., 2005:272, NJ: The Light Inc.

possible by a self that remains focused on the true purpose of its journey. This is why the Divine Trust of selfhood (ego) is a great burden for a human being to carry as it strives to know God and to set his inner heart on Him alone.

While explaining his understanding of the *sama* (whirling), Rumi clearly considers the purpose of the Beloved's breathing into the body, as he replies to the question which he, himself, asks:

> *What is Sama, do you know?*
> *It is hearing the sound of "yes,"*
> *of separating one from himself and reaching the Lord,*
> *Seeing and knowing the state of the Friend and hearing,*
> *through the divine veils, the secrets of the Lord.*

For Rumi, the attraction of all existence, from minute particles to celestial objects, is due to our hidden attraction to the All-Loving. But how are we to know the *Hidden Treasure,* as one feels no zeal toward that which he has never seen or heard of, or about which he knows nothing? In Rumi's words, it is the breath blown into the reed-flute that gives life to it; and it is this breath of the Beloved which we feel within us. Through it, our soul unconsciously carries in itself the innate love for His Essence, which can never be fully contemplated, as nobody can comprehend the Essence of God Himself. How, then, are we to know and love the Rightful Owner of Love?

## KNOW THEN THYSELF

When the ego knows itself, all its limitations and weaknesses, it can gain familiarity with and knowledge of God. The ego can reach the utmost nearness with the Only Beloved if it strives to purify itself. In its raw form, the ego is prone to evil; thus, it needs to be trained and educated by God in order to annihilate the ego and self-centeredness, so as to perfectly align one's will to God. A traveler on the way to God, who is favored with attraction toward God, coming from the Divine Name of the All-Loving, can eventually reach the highest rank of, *the soul in complete rest and satisfaction* (Fajr 89:27).

Referring to this double nature of ego in the opening lines of
a poem, Alexander Pope clearly depicts the self having the free will
to choose either good or evil:

> *Know then thyself, presume not God to scan;*
> *The proper study of mankind is man...*
> *Created half to rise, and half to fall;*
> *Great lord of all things, yet a prey to all...* [4]

Talking of the Divine Trust and "the qualities of fictitious lordship, power and knowledge," which the ego finds in itself, Ünal
states in his translation of the Qur'an, "if the ego forgets the Divine
purpose of its creation, viewing itself as a self-existing being independent of the Creator, it betrays the Trust."[5] Selfhood, then, becomes
so accentuated that its qualities, in time, consist of nothing more
than an ego—the ego being everything. As a result of augmenting
ego over everything, each and every evil-commanding, individual-
istic, material self, especially in our modern times, turns into a "god
within."[6] It shows no inclination toward acknowledging its weaknesses, and conversely assumes to have strength and control over the
things around it. This so-called "modern" ego continually quests
for self-satisfaction and self-adoration as if it were "an idol worthy
of adoration."[7]

However, through its fictitious lordship and power, Ünal says,
the "ego can and must understand the Lordship of the Creator of the
universe."[8] Of all creatures, only human beings have free will. And
by using their free will to make the right choices and, hence, striving to rise to perfection, each ego can truly carry the Divine Trust
when it perceives its own existence as being, "so weak and insub-
stantial that it cannot bear or support anything on its own," and it

---

4    Pope, Alexander, *An Essay on Man*, Opening lines from Epistle II.

5    See Ünal, Ali, *The Qur'an with Annotated Interpretation in Modern English*, 2006:1313-
     16, NJ: The Light Inc.

6    St.Onge, Kathleen, *Bridge to Light*, 2007:48, NJ: The Light Inc.

7    Ünal, ibid., 2006:1316

8    Ibid., 2006:1313.

"renounces its claim to lordship and hypothetical ownership."[9] This way, it acknowledges that its perfection actually lies in its perception of its imperfection and powerlessness. And only through submitting to the Lord of the Worlds, the ego "attains the rank of the best pattern of creation."[10] The ego is, thus, the key to "solving the enigma of creation," as "the Necessarily Existent Being's absolute all-encompassing, and limitless Attributes can become known through it."[11]

Humankind is the most honorable of creatures, and bound by covenant to carry the Divine Trust. Referring to this nature of humanity, with the Trust bestowed on no other creature but humankind, Rumi states:

> *This pure body of ours, our physical being that appears in the form of a human, is the veil of real existence. In fact, we are the qiblah of all those who prostrate.*

> *Do not look at Adam, created of clay, but rather see the breath that was breathed into him and be fascinated by it.*[12]

We feel this proximity to God through this special creation of humankind because "in our self, there is an existence breathed by God. In our self, there is a manifestation of God's manifestation."[13] According to a *hadith qudsi*, God the Almighty says: "I do not fit into the earth and the heavens, but I fit into the heart of my believing servant who loves Me." In his *Gulshan-i Raz* ("The Mystic Rose Garden"), Mahmud Shabstari expresses with amazing beauty how all of existence is a manifestation of God, and nothing in the world can "contain" God save the heart of a faithful servant:

---

[9]  Ibid., p. 1314.

[10]  Ibid., p. 1314.

[11]  Ibid., p. 1313-14.

[12]  Rumi, *Divan-i Kabir*, 3, 1576.

[13]  Quoted in Can, ibid., 2005:257; see also Iqbal, Muhammad, *Armagan-i Hijaz* (Gift from Hijaz), Versified English Translation by Q. A. Kabir, Iqbal Academy Pakistan, Lahore, 1983.

*Know the world is a mirror from head to foot,*
*In every atom a hundred blazing suns.*
*If you cleave the heart of one drop of water,*
*A hundred pure oceans emerge from it...*
*In the wing of a gnat is the ocean of the life,*
*In the pupil of the eye a heaven;*
*What though the grain of the heart be small,*
*It is a station for the Lord of both worlds to dwell therein.*[14]

Thus, knowledge of God is the heart's attainment of friendship with God and the lover's following a way bringing nearness to God. It is the illumined eye of the heart that "sees" the Divine, Who is veiled behind causality. One can, thus, observe the manifestations of Divine Oneness and grasp how a drop is transformed into an ocean and a particle into a sun. One can venture into the depths of the particles and see a solar system embedded in each and every atom.

All existence, indeed, is a manifestation of the light of His Existence. Being aware of this, we can travel between the Divine acts, Names and Attributes and become thrilled with the melodies of belief, the knowledge of God, love, attraction, and the feeling of being attracted by God to Himself. Depending on our devotion and sincere endeavor and through reflecting on the mysteries of His Names and Attributes in and around us we can gain familiarity with and recognition of God. And we can know Him by the rays of the Divine light in the heart through which the *hidden treasury of God* is uncovered.

In another *hadith qudsi*, God the Almighty says that love is the reason for creation, and knowing God is the purpose of life: "I was a *Hidden Treasure* and I loved that I be known, so I created the creation so that I may be known." God reveals Himself in His creation because He wants to be known. And in a Qur'anic verse, the All-Loving says, *"I have not created the jinn and humankind but to worship Me"* (Dhariyat 51:56). Since worshipping Him as if seeing Him

---

14   English translation by E. H. Whinfield

requires knowledge—and thus love of Him—then knowledge of God is the ultimate cause for creation. So, the phrase "to worship Me," in the verse above, can be directly related to the last clause of the *hadith qudsi*, "so that I can be known," as He wills to be known and recognized in the correct way, to be believed and worshipped. So the desire to be known and thus worshipped is hidden in the concept of love.

Speaking to himself in a poem about the Divine Trust, Rumi teaches all of us why we have been journeying from God to this guesthouse of the world, while using a shocking pun on the Arabic word *balâ*:

> He asked: "Am I not your Lord?" And you responded: "Balâ" (Yes)!
> How can one thank Him for that "balâ" (yes)? By balâ (suffering
> misfortunes)![15]

## SUFFERING AND THE REED'S SEPARATION IN SEPARATION

There is nothing more bitter than parting from the Beloved, and the reed-flute feels and knows this separation in its conscience of its native land. Thus, it longs for reunion, always sighing when it recollects the reed-bed. By this allegory, Rumi refers to a human being's innate feeling of the covenant in his conscience, as well as his quest for God after being sent to the world. While singing wistfully and longing to return to the Source, like the lover passionately longing for the Beloved, the reed-flute harbors the essence of nostalgia, as Rumi says in another couplet: "Although bodily water and clay have cast skepticism upon us, something of those melodies comes back to our memory."[16]

Though the separation Rumi felt after reaching contentment in the knowledge of God is unbearable, he consoles himself with the thought that this separation is the requirement of being on the way to the Beloved, from Whom he has been separated but has

---

[15]  Rumi, *Divan-i Kabir*, *Ghazal* No: 251, 2818, for the pun see also Kuşpınar, B., "The Concept of Man" p.5.
[16]  Rumi, *Masnavi*, Vol. IV, 737.

pledged to meet with purity in the realm where souls fly. For Rumi, it is, "the sorrow that guides us."[17] In various poems, he likens suffering and sorrow to a guest knocking on the door, who tries to see beyond it, who seeks to enter through this door half-opened in the heart.

The reed is well aware that any pain or sorrow a traveler bears on the way to the Beloved is sweet in itself, for all sorrows and joys felt on the way to Him are because of Him and from Him. It sees separation as living in the realm between spirituality and pure materialism so that it can attain the Beloved in the end. Its parting is with Him, its union is with Him, and the cure for its suffering is also with Him, as it cries out in frenzy: "Who saw like the reed-flute in grief yet with the cure in its pain?" Thus, Rumi's lament over separation is not a complaint of his ego; rather, it is like the great contemporary Islamic scholar, Said Nursi's, seeking of the love of God:

> *I have found the True Beloved;*
> *Ah, I suffered much pain because of separation.*[18]

This suffering of separation that humankind has to undergo in maintaining the Trust is crowned with the love of the Beloved. One's finding God is, by itself, the lover's union with the Beloved—a union in the state of separation. Of Rumi, Muhammad Iqbal says, "there is sorrow, a burning that is not strange to us. His union talks of going beyond the separations. One feels the beauty of love in his reed and receives a share, a blessing from the Greatness of God."[19] Despite his suffering from separation, Rumi is thankful for his crazed love as he is intoxicated with the wine of love. He never complains of burning with His love, but seeks instead an increase in the fervor of Divine love.

Multi-level reading is a must while listening to this reed. Though Rumi endures this separation, no matter how difficult it is, he goes

---

17   Rumi, *Fihi Ma Fihi*.
18   Nursi, Bediüzzaman Said, *The Words*, 2005:232, NJ: The Light Inc.
19   Quoted in Can, ibid., 2005:265; see also Iqbal, Muhammad, ibid., 1983.

through a second and still more difficult separation which he must deal with, because Rumi himself—as a man advanced in divine intoxication—most suffers when he is among those unaware of spirituality. Though the reed's plaintive music fills the eyes of all men and women with tears, as expressed in the second couplet of the poem, their spirits do not hear the lover's sorrowful wails of separation. They never go beyond the surface level of things, and being obsessed only with the appearance, they cannot help but shed tears only upon gazing at the reed's suffering. However, Rumi is looking for other hearts like his own, hearts *"torn, torn from separation,"* so that he may share the pain of lamentation. And this is, in a sense, a separation in which Rumi finds himself–the separation by which a righteous man of knowledge and discernment finds himself among those who restrict themselves only to the outward senses without perceiving and observing with the heart. This heedlessness of theirs is a torment within a torment, a separation in a separation.

> They have hearts with which they do not seek the essence of matters to grasp the truth, and they have eyes with which they do not see, and they have ears with which they do not hear... Those are the unmindful and heedless. (A'raf 7:179)

Thus, it is not really with the physical eyes or outward senses that man can see; instead, it is only with the Light of the Beloved, to Whom belong all Beautiful Names.

This great saint suffers remoteness in parallel with his nearness, no matter how much he moans and cries *"in every company."* None seeks, in Rumi's words, *"to discover the secrets within me."* Though Rumi's secret is manifest *"in the notes"* he wails, it is the fate of such great persons as Rumi that people around them are not aware of their spiritual profundity. Rather they become friendly with them *"according to their fancy."*

As Rumi seeks his spiritual contentment in the happiness of others, in the light of the Qur'anic verse, *company with them in this world kindly* (Luqman 31:15), he tries to lead them to *follow the way of those who turn to Me (in love)* (Luqman 31:15). So, tasting the pleasure of knowledge of God and the wine of Divine love, Rumi longs for nothing but nearness to the Beloved; and attaining His friendship and company, he always seeks to find a way to penetrate the hearts of those around him, so that they may join him on the journey and reap its immeasurable rewards.

This can be seen even more clearly and directly when the reed-flute's plaintive tunes end and Rumi begins his commentary in couplet nine. Here, he prays for those of his audience whose sensual ears and eyes are not able to discern what the spiritual world offers: *"May he be naught if he be lacking this fervent desire for fire."* Here, Rumi prays for them to come to know separation's torment like himself, and hence experience self-annihilation so that they can attain proximity with the Beloved. This suffering is necessary for any wayfarer dedicated to attaining a spiritual life. This is why Rumi advises men of affliction to swallow poison as if it were sweet from the very hands of the Beloved for the lover: *"It's the ferment of love in this wine enrapturing."* It seems that he wants men of affliction to be pleased with the idea that their sufferings are not bound to come to an end until death, which is when the door will open onto the "World of Spirit," for the reunion after separation. In this way, he wants all travelers to God to strive to purify themselves, to discover their inner heart in which there exists the "Hidden Treasure," and then to lead a life at the level of the heart.

RUMI'S SECRET OF SECRETS

Rumi's secret is his degree of relationship with the Beloved, a sacred secret rising in his heart, kept hidden from the view of others. While being wishful to reveal this secret of him to kindle the flame of His love in the hearts of others, Rumi humbly conceals his self instead and speaks in the voice of his central metaphor of the reed-flute, whose *"wailing tones shred the shroud of the hearts veiled."*

The allegorical style which Rumi demonstrates in the Song of the Reed operates beyond merely serving an aesthetic purpose. Feeling astonished at the burning manifestations of His Face, the poetic genius mentions about his love of Him with allegories not only in

his *Masnavi* but in his other works, as well. In doing so, he expresses his being favored with the burning manifestations of Divine
Existence in the language of men, leaving no room for any misunderstanding. In his *Divan-i Kabir*, for instance, his reed-flute, for whom
the Flutist is manifest, becomes "drunk from the wine of His lips…Such
a sigh, because of this sweet-songed reed-breaking Flutist!"[20] The
heart of the body is, in Rumi's words, disturbed with the Divine
manifestations as it feels that there is a Disturber. Feeling attracted
by God with a continuously increasing force, Rumi lives in excessive joy and with great happiness and ecstasy. As a result, his body
cannot help but break itself in the sight of such reflections, as beautifully expressed elsewhere in *Masnavi*:

> *When you seek love, by the grace of God*
> *Your spirit turns into wine and your body into a jar.*
> *When He increases the wine of His grace, the jar falls into pieces.*
> *Every knowledgeable one knows without thinking,*
> *That where there is disturbance, there is a Disturber.*[21]

Through His grace and favors, Rumi has become both enlightened and enlightening—a universal person. Rumi, held in such
Divine attraction, cannot help but feel Divine compassion poured
into his inner body. However, he shows his humility and his understanding of nothingness, while keeping his inner world pure, as he
delivers his spiritual profundity through the lowly reed, thereby
avoiding the direct display of his own inward riches. And he does
his best to keep God's special favors to him as sacred "secrets" between
himself and his Beloved in his "Talks on the Beloved"[22] through
symbols and metaphors. Thus, while exposing his own heart in his
address to the audience through the voice of the reed, Rumi simultaneously conceals the blessings he is given throughout the song of
the reed, so as to direct the attention to the "song" rather than to the

---

20  Rumi, *Divan-i Kabir, Ghazal* No: 1936.
21  Rumi, *Masnavi*, Vol. III, 4743-44, 4749.
22  Making every effort constantly to draw attention to Him, Rumi would call his gath-
    erings, 'Talks on the Beloved.'

singer. The wistful singing of the reed pours out Rumi's heart, and thus it makes the eyes of the human heart wide open to his secret. This is clearly what Rumi wishes! He hopes that people in an immature spiritual condition will be aroused with the internal need to refine their selves through various levels of training, so that they might undergo a change of character by which they might be helped in attaining a "second nature," thus allowing them to become transformed into perfected humans. So, this great counselor and healer aims to raise the awareness in us that we are the most precious creation of God. And once we sense His breath in us and explore how much we need to love the True Beloved, then the secrets of the Divine will begin to be revealed to us. Rumi is looking—in order for these secrets to be known—for those who have similar longings and complaints, who have such experience of the heart *"torn, torn from separation"* as stated more clearly in one of his *ghazals*:

> My heart, be seated near that person who has experience of the heart,
> Go under that tree which bears fresh blossoms.[23]

While sipping cup-by-cup from the wine of Divine love, having to live every moment of his life among people of the corporeal world, on the one hand, is like sipping poison for Rumi. On the other hand, since he is very sincere in his exclusive devotion to the Beloved, he wants to stir up the same feelings in others and arouse in hearts the desire for burning with the love of the Beloved. Beyond considering that he has been made to experience sufferings, he welcomes such sufferings and has become intoxicated with the pleasure thus received. He finds an antidote for poison in the poison itself—peace and coolness in the fervor of love, joyfully desiring of it more and more, with the pleasure of feeling God's company. Thus, beyond revealing his secret, he wishes to share his love for the Beloved with those whose hearts are bleeding and torn open with longing— those who are in grief and yet hold the cure in their pain.

---

23  Rumi, *Divan-i Kabir, Ghazal* No. 563.

Again, taking the advantage of the permissibility of the metaphor of the crazed lover, *Majnun*, the legendary personality of passionate love, Rumi expresses his state of intoxication during which he loses himself due to the depth of his love for the Beloved, as the breezes of nearness to Him begin to blow with God's surprising visit to the heart, reminding this lover of God that the door of the Beloved is ajar.

In relation to the reed's "telling of the beloved for whom *Majnun's* heart bled," Rumi refers more directly to *"the way stained with blood"* in a *ghazal*:

> *I am like Majnun in my poor heart, which is without limbs,*
> *Because I have no strength to contest the love of God.*
>
> *Every day and night, I continue in my efforts to free myself*
> *From the bonds of the chain of love; a chain that keeps me imprisoned.*
>
> *When the dream of the Beloved begins, I find myself in blood.*
> *Because I am not*
> *Fully conscious, I am afraid in that I may paint Him with the blood*
> *of my heart.*

Rumi lived among the people as one of them, and being a man, he used the language of men. Showing his humility, he likened himself to *Majnun* to allude to his love for the Divine Beloved. Once he is God-intoxicated, he becomes, in his words, "not fully conscious," as his love for the Beloved is beyond description:

> *Love is reckless; not reason.*
> *Reason seeks a profit.*
> *There is no one more insane than the lover*
> *For his reason is blind and deaf because of love.*[24]

Thus, Rumi is overpowered by Divine love, as his heart boils with excessive joy and excitement whenever he feels himself approached indescribably nearer to the Beloved. Since the real

---

[24]  Rumi, *Masnavi*, Vol. VI, 1966-67.

panacea is to see *"the Face of God,"* in whatever direction the lovers turn (Baqara 2:115), this sultan of lovers feels fully surrounded by His signs. He finds himself in the state of full intoxication with the wine of love and is enraptured by the rays of the manifestations of the Beloved's "Face," as the veil between the lover and the Beloved is partly lifted so that the way to union shows itself to some degree. He captures the sentiment exactly in a poem: "This is love: to fly toward a secret sky, to cause a hundred veils to fall each moment."[25] Being God-intoxicated, he then explains why he cannot help but disclose his secret in answering the question, "How is it that the mirror reveals nothing?" For it is as if "love wants these words to manifest."[26] So, the more Rumi wishes to avoid publicizing his secret, the more love speaks out as it is not the lover talking but the love itself that raises its head and says, "I am here!" Rumi expresses this intoxicating love incredibly beautifully in a quatrain,

> *Love is here like the blood in my veins and skin.*
> *It has emptied me of myself and filled me with the Beloved,*
> *His fire has penetrated all the atoms of my body*
> *Of "me" only my name remains; the rest is Him.*

Rumi feels himself in the most pleasurable state of being freed even from his name and his existence. For Rumi, the fervor of Divine love burns away worldly forms. Due to love, as Rumi says in another couplet in his *Masnavi*, nothing is left in him save the Beloved: "Love is that flame which, when it blazes up, burns everything except the Beloved."[27]

## JOURNEYING WITH, OR IN THE COMPANY OF, THE BELOVED

Rumi has a heart that falls in love with the All-Beloved and is invaded by ecstasies. Thus, he lives wonder-struck and feels deeply the com-

---

25  Rumi, *Divan-i Kabir, Ghazal* No. 13.
26  Rumi, *Masnavi*, Vol. I, 33.
27  Rumi, ibid., Vol. V, 588.

pany of the Beloved. Self-annihilated in His company, living unaware of himself and filled with wonder, Rumi's heart gains familiarity with the mysteries and lights of the Beloved's company.

In "the Song of the Reed," the reed expresses the favor of the Flutist's company through the excitement of feeling the Flutist's breath that burns away the reed in its intense flames of love. It knows that the beauty of the tune in the plaintive notes, in fact, comes from the breathing of the Flutist. While seeking union with the Beloved, the reed has actually been recollecting the breath of the Beloved at every moment into the complete forgetfulness of itself. In another word, it annihilates itself in the Breather, emptying the body in the pain of parting from the Breather so that it fills its transient self completely with the tunes of the Flutist. Of itself, there remains only a hollow and finger holes; everything else is the Breather. This is because, in the words of Rumi; "We are as the flute, and the music in us is from Thee."[28] Elsewhere he says: "Be empty of stomach and cry out, in neediness, like the reed-flute!"[29]

The feeling of powerlessness and neediness, as well as wonder and astonishment over the reed's music, arouses in others a burning desire to set out for the meeting with the Beloved. Hence, once individuals have the realization of their powerlessness in God's Presence at every moment, they can get out of their ego traps and become detached from their existence, like the reed-flute. By feeling the transience of their own attributes, these lovers then taste the pleasure of permanence in the Attributes of God, and subsequently take a further step toward attaining His company. For the lovers, attainment of this rank brings with it a feeling of wonder, intoxication and astonishment. These lovers, who have acquired the rank of *the soul in complete rest and satisfaction* (Fajr 89:27), finally find the greatest peace and happiness in this feeling of the company of God, and experience the pleasure of intimacy with Him.

---

28  Rumi, ibid., Vol. I, 599.
29  Rumi, *Divan-i Kabir, Ghazal* No: 1739.

Though the *"reunion is held up"* as the days draw out for the
lover, as stated in couplet fifteen of the Song of the Reed, Rumi does
not care for the *"days gone"* with the suffering of separation, so long
as the Beloved stays in company, as declared in the next couplet,
where God is addressed directly: *"You remain, O You Pure One."*

Rumi then likens the lovers to the fish in the next couplet. Here
he refers to lovers whose thirst is deepened by drinking, neither
quenched nor satisfied. They are those who are deeply in love with
the Beloved and therefore drown with wonder and spiritual pleasures in the Divine manifestations which pervade the heart during
the journey. Once they have been submerged in the ocean of Divine
love even once, they can no longer live without the water of the
ocean of love. In Rumi's words, *"Only the fish drowning in water
grow thirstier."*

Since it is only the heart of the lover that can contain the Beloved,
the more the inner heart of the lover imbibes in the depths of the
manifestations of the Beloved, the more it petitions for His gifts.
The thirst of the yearning lover increases more and more until his
heart overflows with love and burns away in flames. Through this
analogy in the poem, Rumi clearly expresses that he feels pleasure
embedded in this yearning, and satisfaction embedded in the
unquenchable thirst of longing for more and more of the ferment
of love. Rumi is swept up in the spiritual pleasures, amazement and
astonishment that pervade his whole being.

The days of those without Rumi's experience of the heart *"grow
longer,"* like the lovers whose *"days grow, lengthening,"* but with a
major difference in that these lovers are God-intoxicated in the company of the Beloved, whereas the others have not yet drunk the wine
of love from the Beloved's lips. This is why Rumi keeps in company with them and wishes them to have the heart "torn, torn from
separation," so that they can also drink the wine of love and breathe
the breezes of being in the Beloved's company, thus becoming *people whom He loves, and who love Him* (Maidah 6:54). As he loves
everything for His sake; he fervently desires to sacrifice his life for

others, *out of love for Him* (Baqara 2:177). And he does his best to "be friendly with everyone, and carve a friend out of stone."[30]

Ultimately, Rumi wishes only that people will love Him Whom he loves, and he hopes that the only thing they will ever discuss is his Beloved. He even comes out asking the audience challengingly, *"Who saw like the reed-flute, a longing lover and a true companion?"* In this, he seeks the firm attention of all people so that they might *"listen to this reed-flute."* Thus, Rumi becomes a remote star, "neither of the East, nor of the West,"[31] his presence equally felt in the past and present, like a shining light on the entire globe throughout the ages, illuminating everyone in direct proportion to the accessibility of their hearts.

Thus, Rumi uses his poetic talent in the best way possible, in the service of God, to kindle the flame of divine love in the inner heart, the station of the Lord of all the worlds, *wherein His name is oft-remembered.* (Nur 24:36) In order to inspire our transformation, his central metaphor of the sweet-songed reed acts like a clear and pure reflection for the manifestation of the Beloved's Light, like a lamp in a *crystal shining, as if a pearl-like radiant star, lit from the oil of a blessed olive tree that is neither of the east nor of the west* (Nur 24:35). And in return for his keeping company with everyone, the All-Merciful assigns for Rumi a profound love in the hearts of many people so that he receives countless blessings from them (Maryam 19:96). Yet, for those to whom this God-intoxicated lover's unconsciousness only appears as madness, Rumi's last word is, *"farewell!"*

---

30  Rumi, *Masnavi*, Vol. VI, 2154.

31  See R.A. Nicholson translation, *Selected Poems from the Divan-i Shamsi Tabriz*, Cambridge University Press, 1977.

# Rumi's Seven Pieces of Advice

In generosity and helping others

*be like the river.*

In compassion and grace

*be like the sun.*

In concealing others' faults

*be like the night.*

In anger and fury

*be like the dead.*

In modesty and humility

*be like the soil.*

In tolerance

*be like the ocean.*

Either appear as you are or

*be as you appear.*

# Maxims from Rumi

"The wars of men are like the quarrels of children;
            both are meaningless and stupid."

"Indeed envy is a defect, worse than any other."

"If you want to receive mercy, be merciful to the weak."

"Before you say anything, first listen."

"Thoughtless friends are themselves the enemy."

"Don't allow your animal nature to rule your reason."

"The people of the world don't examine themselves,
            and so they blame one another."

"O, happy is the soul that sees its own faults."

"The middle path is the way to wisdom."

"Revile those who flatter you."

"The essence of all wisdom is to know the answers to 'who am I?'
and 'what will become of me?' on the Day of Judgment."

"Know that a word suddenly shot from the tongue is like an arrow
shot from the bow. Son, that arrow won't turn back on its way;
you must damn the torrent at its source."

"Look where you step. You will avoid a false step
            and you will be saved from stumbling."

"The carnal soul inside you that is waiting to ambush you is
worse than anything else in terms of pride and resentment."

"Hard work and earning are not obstacles to finding a treasure!
Continue to work hard, if it is God's will, the treasure will find you."

# INDEX